PLANTS
for
SMALL
SPACES

PLANTS
for
SMALL
SPACES

STEPHANIE
DONALDSON
— *&* —
SUSAN
BERRY

COLLINS & BROWN

Plants for Small Spaces
First published in Great Britain in 1998 by Collins & Brown Limited
London House Great Eastern Wharf Parkgate Road London SW11 4NQ

135798642

British Library Cataloguing-in-Publication Data:
A catalogue record for this book is available from the British Library.

ISBN 1 85585 471 6 (hardback edition)
ISBN 1 85585 645 X (paperback edition)

A BERRY BOOK
Conceived, edited and designed by Susan Berry for Collins & Brown Limited

Editor Jane Struthers
Section Editors Alison Freegard and Amanda Lebentz
Executive Editor Ginny Surtees

Designer Roger Daniels
Managing Art Editor Kevin Williams

Photography Michelle Garrett, Howard Rice and Steven Wooster

Reproduction by Hong Kong Graphic & Printing Ltd.
Printed and bound in Hong Kong by Dai Nippon Printing Co.

Contents

INTRODUCTION

We have all used the phrase 'small is beautiful' at one time or another and this is certainly the effect we strive for when gardening in small spaces. By using the vertical as well as the horizontal surfaces you can greatly increase the potential planting areas, and the addition of raised containers will allow vertical planting away from the

boundaries. With gardening on this scale, every inch is precious and good seasonal planting is needed to ensure there is colour and interest throughout the year. Even the tiniest space needs drama, as well as good plantings, and the inclusion of a large pot with a striking plant, a column, or a statue will create a focal point to complete the design of your small, but beautiful, space.

ABOVE *Even steps can provide an ideal place for planting, as this complementary group of scented herbs, busy Lizzies, chrysanthemums and fuchsia demonstrates.*

RIGHT *Not an inch of space is lost for planting on this small terrace, with its wonderful display of summer-flowering annuals, including scented tobacco plants, petunias and lobelia, many in raised containers.*

THE CHALLENGE OF gardening in a small space lies in using the limited area as effectively as possible to create the kind of garden that suits you and your lifestyle. All the ideas in this book are easily achievable and there is no structural work involved, beyond putting up a hook for a hanging basket, but there are lots of inspiring ideas to help you transform the garden you have into the garden you want. *Plants for Small Spaces* introduces you to a range of planting concepts that will help you get the most out of your garden by using all the surfaces available to you. Walls, windowsills, doorways, steps, corners, the terraced patio or the balcony – all can be adorned with plants that trail, climb or spread from pots, troughs and hanging baskets. Container planting is an essential element of gardening in a small space, and you will find plenty of inspiration for every shape and size of container, as well as practical advice on how to be a successful container gardener.

The final section of this book, the Plant Finder, will help you to select suitable plants for the conditions in your garden, plants that will perform well throughout

ABOVE *The architectural beauty of topiary plants contrasts interestingly with the informal background.*

the year, fill your garden with colour, shape and

texture, and enable you to achieve the overall effect

you desire. The great bonus of gardening in a small

space is that it allows you time – time to experiment, to

plan and to sit and enjoy the fruits of your labour. Don't

envy those with larger gardens – time is a luxury they

seldom enjoy.

BELOW *Shade is no obstacle to planting small spaces: busy Lizzies in an antique wire container, hostas, little blue creeping campanulas, purple-leaved* Heuchera *and a host of other foliage plants are crammed together in a richly textured tapestry.*

PLANTING CONCEPTS

Plants play many roles in the garden but in a small

space the planting schemes, and combinations of

plants, have to be carefully chosen to ensure they

perform to greatest effect. Background colour,

instant effects, seasonal variety and vertical, as well

as horizontal, plantings are all ways in which to get

the most from your plants

and keep your space

looking colourful through-

out the seasons. Also,

different forms of plants

can be used for different situations and surfaces.

ABOVE *Neatly clipped topiary box balls provide a textural and architectural contrast with blowzy lilies. The elegant striped pots in blue and white emphasize the arrangement.*

RIGHT *Formality plays an important role in small-space planting, its architectural shapes a foil for more ephemeral seasonal flower colour.*

ABOVE *Handsome foliage plants make a welcome change from bright flowers, and create a useful focal point.*

FACING PAGE *Planting in tiers, using attractive terracotta and metal raised containers, makes maximum use of available space and creates the illusion of a much larger garden.*

*I*N GENERAL, THERE *are two approaches to planting. There is the rational approach, in which the gardener allows the space to dictate the planting, and the acquisitive approach, embodied by the gardener who yearns to grow a particular plant and will find a way to fit it into the available space. The rational gardener enjoys formal gardening and appreciates controlled colour schemes and symmetry, while the acquisitive gardener is more at home with the informal style of garden plants where colour is riotous, plants climb or sprawl, and the design evolves more by happy accident than planning. You will find gardening more fulfilling if you decide at the outset which approach most appeals to you. If you long for a miniature Versailles, love topiary and prefer single-colour schemes, you are a rationalist who will enjoy planning your garden on paper and will have the patience to train plants. If, on the other hand, you love impulse buying and like to experiment, then you are an acquisitive gardener who will enjoy an informal garden. Once you have decided which category suits you, you will have some guidelines to work within. For instance, vertical planting in the formal garden should be largely evergreen with flowering plants as accent colour, while the informal garden benefits from a colourful succession of flowers.*

VERTICAL PLANTING

In the short term, pots and planters may be used to decorate walls and fences in a small garden, but they are fairly labour-intensive and the better long-term solution is to plant your boundaries with a selection of climbing plants. A combination of climbers will provide year-round interest.

THERE ARE many beautiful climbers that will happily intertwine and provide a succession of glorious flowers and foliage to brighten the gloomiest corner or the dullest wall. Although most climbing plants prefer to be positioned where they enjoy some sunshine, it is surprising how many, including some varieties of roses, honeysuckle and clematis, as well as ivy, will thrive on a shady wall (see pages 120-1).

The key to growing climbing plants successfully on walls and fences in a small garden is the careful choice of suitable varieties and good soil preparation, followed by regular feeding and pruning. It is possible to grow climbing plants in large containers, although they will do better and need less attention if they are planted in the ground. A surprisingly small area is needed: for instance, a bed of just 30×60cm (1×2ft) was needed for the honeysuckle (*Lonicera*) and potato vine (*Solanum crispum* 'Glasnevin') in the main picture. This same bed also contained a climbing rose which had flowered earlier in the season, with an underplanting of lilies and rosemary.

TOP *Clematis* 'The Vagabond' *twines with a star jasmine* (Trachelospermum diffusum).

ABOVE *Boston ivy* (Parthenocissus tricuspidata) *or Virginia creeper* (P. quinquefolia) *will rapidly cover a brick wall, without the need for any supports. It makes an ideal backdrop for more colourful displays in containers.*

LEFT *A black-painted fence with horizontal wire supports is the backdrop for a lush summer display of pink* 'New Dawn' *roses and mauve clematis* 'Prince Charles'.

FACING PAGE *This planting of honeysuckle and potato vine in contrasting yellows and purples ensures a long-lasting display.*

FOCAL POINTS

Whether you know it or not, your garden already has a focal point – the point to which the eye naturally travels when entering or viewing the garden. If you are lucky this will be something attractive – possibly a tree, an architectural plant or a statue. Yet unattractive features can draw the eye just as powerfully and may need to be removed, disguised or supplanted by a different, more pleasing focal point before the full potential of the garden can be realized.

DEPENDING ON the size and shape of your garden, you may have more than one focal point. Generally speaking, any clearly defined area should have a single focal point and this is determined by looking at the area from the most used viewpoint – attempting to create other focal points from different viewpoints can result in a rather muddled, over-busy effect. It doesn't matter that viewing the focal point from different aspects may not reveal it in its full glory; this adds an element of mystery to the garden and encourages the observer to explore it further. Some of the most successful gardens rely on this type of effect.

If the view beyond your boundaries is worth looking at, you can add distance and perspective to your focal point by raising it and framing it against a backdrop of the view beyond. For instance, you can place a statue or urn on a plinth rather than leave it at ground level. This immediately gives the object increased visual importance. Alternatively, you can plant a group of taller, flowering

shrubs behind the statue or urn to draw the eye upwards. Conversely, if the view over the fence leaves a lot to be desired, then the focal point should be at a low level to encourage the eye away from the offending blot on the landscape. A pond or other water feature is particularly effective, especially if it includes

some running water which is usually an irresistible draw. This adds another dimension to your garden and creates a very tranquil effect that is particularly refreshing in the hot summer months.

In many small spaces one of the most important functions of a focal point is to add height to what can sometimes be a rather flat plane. This can be done by creating a point of interest on a wall, by playing with scale and including a large architectural feature, or through the use of topiary. At night-time, some well positioned lighting will add further drama to the scene.

In a garden with no obvious focal point you can locate the most effective position by placing a fairly tall object, such as a step-ladder, at various points around the garden until you find the position that has the most interesting effect on the shape and perspective of the garden. This will be your focal point.

LEFT *This statue of a young girl draws the eye through the layers of plants in a mixed herbaceous border. She is surrounded by phlox and balsam (Impatiens balsamina) flowers.*

BELOW *Even a hedge can form a backdrop to a focal point. Here, an alcove has been cut in the hedge to provide a home for a stone bust. This creates a sense of mystery and surprise for the visitor who may not notice the piece of statuary at first. In the winter, when the herbaceous border dies back, the stone bust will be revealed in all its splendour.*

LEFT *A shady bower has been created from some trelliswork which allows you to see into the garden beyond while creating a backdrop to the ornate metal seating. The bower is completed by the stone mask which hangs from the top of the trellis.*

RIGHT *The base of a tree forms the focal point for a statue and a mixed summer planting of petunias, marguerites, agapanthus and helichrysum. All these plants are in containers that can be removed when the flowering display is over. In this way, you can create different plantings for each season.*

WIGWAM FOR CLIMBERS

Tall-growing, colourful plants are an important element in a small garden because they provide height. Wall plants such as roses (Rosa), clematis (Clematis) and honeysuckle (Lonicera) will form the backdrop, but you can enjoy wonderful additional colour with climbing annuals such as sweet peas (Lathyrus odoratus), nasturtiums (Tropaeolum), morning glories (Ipomoea) and even runner beans (Phaseolus) planted in large pots and encouraged to clamber up twiggy sticks.

ALTHOUGH sweet peas (*Lathyrus odoratus*) are sometimes available in the shops in summer as cut flowers, it is rare for them to be as richly scented as the garden-grown varieties. Growing a pot of sweet peas will provide a double pleasure – fragrance and colour in the garden and a prolific supply of cut flowers.

Traditionally, sweet peas were grown in straight rows in very fertile soil in the kitchen garden. Side-shoots were ruthlessly pinched out and only the finest, straightest-stalked blooms were allowed to reach maturity. Plant breeders concentrated on developing large blooms at the cost of fragrance and there was eventually a danger that these lovely flowers would become insipid, overblown shadows of their glorious ancestors. Fortunately there is a real revival of interest in the old varieties and it is once again easy to buy sweet pea seeds or young plants in which colour and fragrance are given equal importance.

Sweet peas grow surprisingly well in large pots provided that they are planted in good potting compost enriched with composted stable manure. A regular liquid feed will ensure a long flowering period, which will also be encouraged by picking the flowers as soon as they have opened. If flowers are left to set seed on the plants the flowering season will be much shorter.

Most annual climbers require similar treatment, although nasturtiums are the exception. They do better in poor soil.

HOW TO GROW SWEET PEAS IN A POT

You can use ordinary 1.5m (5ft) garden canes to support sweet peas grown in a pot, but twiggy sticks will look more decorative and the sweet peas will be able to clamber through them without the aid of plant rings. A 40cm (16in) pot is roomy enough for 10-12 plants spaced evenly around the edge of the pot. Sweet peas grow well from seed. The seeds are large and easy to handle. Plant them in a 15cm (6in) diameter pot about 1cm (1/2in) deep and 1cm (1/2in) apart. Put the pot in good light and keep moist. When they are about 8cm (3in) tall, they can be transplanted to the larger pot and supported with canes or sticks.

1 *Take a large pot and cover the base with broken shards of pot to create a drainage layer before partially filling with compost.*

2 *Transfer the sweet pea seedlings to the large pot, positioning them around the edge. Fill with compost nearly to the top.*

3 *Firmly push the twigs or canes into position between the evenly spaced sweet pea plants.*

4 *Tie the twigs or canes together to form a wigwam. Canes will only need tying at the top, whereas twigs may need more restraint. Water well.*

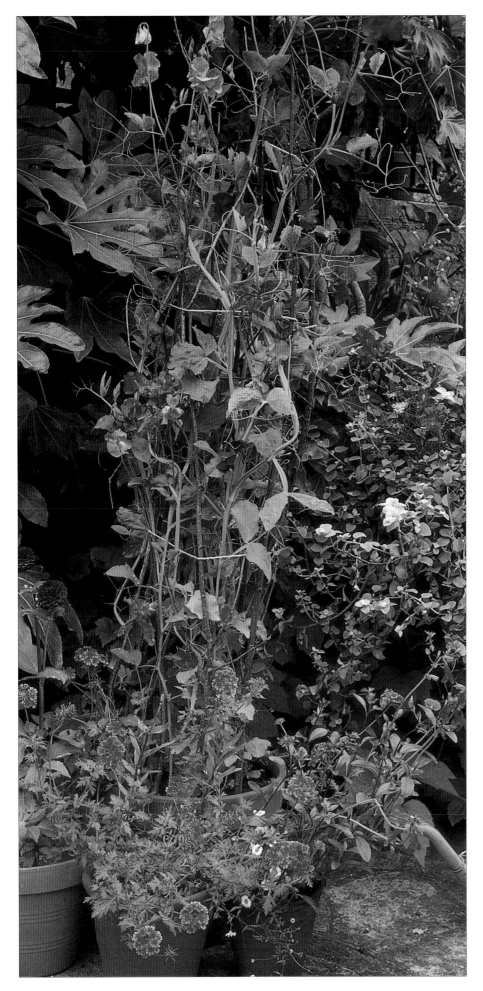

LEFT *Be sure to position your sweet peas where you can best enjoy their beauty and fragrance. A sunny, sheltered corner where you like to sit is ideal, or next to a path or French windows where the scent will stop you in your tracks.*

ABOVE *Picking sweet peas encourages the plants to keep flowering. At the height of the summer you will be able to pick flowers every day, although as the season progresses the stems will get shorter and shorter.*

SEASONAL DISPLAYS

Gardening in small spaces is at its best when there is a succession of plantings throughout the year. These need not be elaborate or expensive – two or three containers filled with plants in their prime are all that is needed to transform what may otherwise be a rather gloomy winter garden. Similarly, a group of pots planted with miniature bulbs placed on a wall or table will entice you out into the early spring sunshine to admire their beauty and fragrance.

THE GARDEN, terrace or balcony can, if you choose, undergo a transformation each season. Although impulse buying when plants are flowering is not generally recommended during the summer when the result is often very short-lived plants, buying plants this way during the cooler months allows you to assemble instant displays that will last well.

At the same time, a little planning can ensure colour throughout the year. Bulbs planted under herbaceous plants in the autumn will provide fresh colour in the spring when the herbaceous plants are starting to send out green shoots. During the summer and autumn months, colourful annuals and half-hardy perennials will provide strong colour in containers and fill any gaps in the borders. Evergreen and fruiting or berried shrubs and climbers will give colour and structure to the garden throughout the autumn and winter.

You can have some containers that you earmark for changing displays, replanting them each season. This is almost always the case with window-boxes, since if this is your entire gardening space, you cannot simply move the containers to a more out of the way spot when the plants are past their best. Such a scheme could involve cyclamens, heathers and winter-flowering pansies

in the colder months; small scillas, primulas and dwarf narcissi in the spring; verbena or helichyrsum with trailing diascias and pelargoniums in the summer; and chrysanthemums with pernettya and small foliage plants in autumn. With a terrace or small backyard at your disposal you can have more permanent seasonal displays, simply moving containers into the foreground or background, as the state of their planting dictates.

LEFT AND ABOVE *Troughs and smaller containers filled with tulips and other spring flowers add instant colour to a dark corner in the garden.*

TOP, ABOVE AND RIGHT *Hanging baskets, windowboxes and other containers do not have to look subdued in the winter months. A windowbox of purple ornamental cabbages and pink heathers (top) makes a vivid splash of autumn colour, while a hanging basket of mixed pansies and primulas (above and right) looks cheerful in early spring.*

INSTANT EFFECTS

Although long-term planning is generally advised in gardening, there are times when you simply can't wait. Maybe the garden needs transforming for a special party, the summer border flowered early in the season and is now lacking colour, or a house move means you have inherited a rather dull garden which needs brightening up while you make long-term plans. Whatever the reason, planted containers can create an instant change of scene.

FOR A SMALL GARDEN to look its best consistently, you need to emphasize the plants that are looking good and disguise those that aren't. This can be done with groupings of container plants set against a backdrop of structural plants growing in borders and up walls and fences. You can then bring plants to the fore as they come into flower and tuck those that are past their best into the background. Planted in containers of different sizes and heights, a group of herbaceous plants can create an instant summer border, and when underplanted with bulbs they also provide spring colour. Many evergreens grow happily in pots and can be used to provide year-round colour even when not in flower. Evergreen variegated plants are very useful because they can add depth and interest to a group of plants that might otherwise look rather dull. With a core collection of shrubs and perennials you can then add colour with annuals and half-hardy perennials.

Moving large containers can be heavy work, so choose a fairly permanent position for these and only move them when a complete change of scene is called for. However, you should get into the habit of moving the smaller containers around frequently. You don't need to move them all, just two or three at a time will create a constantly changing view.

Be bold for that special occasion. Get help and move all the containers around to give a change of focus, then spend some time tidying, weeding and trimming so that each plant looks its best. Choose a colour scheme and go for it in a big way using blocks of colour – two or three containers densely planted with a single colour will make much more impact than a mixed planting.

LEFT AND ABOVE *At first glance, the border (left) appears to be a richly planted herbaceous bed in its full summer glory. Tobacco plants, helichrysum, Lysimachia, rosemary and penstemon are all flowering their hearts out while a golden hop clambers up a piece of trellis. The photograph above reveals the truth – the plants are in carefully arranged containers while foliage hides the pots and creates the impression of a planted border.*

RIGHT AND FAR RIGHT *You can buy flowering plants and bulbs from a garden centre and create instant displays in the early spring. This wooden tub has been planted with daffodils, white Dicentra and hyacinths.*

FORMS OF CONTAINER

When gardening in a small space the container is king – it gives the garden flexibility and allows for transformations that would not be possible if all planting was in the soil. Each container is in effect a miniature garden with its own soil conditions, climate and aspect, all of which you can control. Whether

positioned singly or grouped to create layers of planting, containers make up the furniture of the garden, without which the space can look bare and incomplete.

ABOVE *Chrysanthemums and lilies fill a small plant stand, creating a colourful focal point.*

RIGHT *Decorated terracotta and wooden pots and a rustic wooden trug all help to create variety and interest in small space gardening.*

*T*HE DAYS WHEN *container gardening meant choosing between a terracotta and a plastic flowerpot are gone. Even the most basic garden centre now has a good range of competitively priced pots, troughs and planters to choose from, while specialist craftsmen and importers will supply you with anything from amazingly authentic-looking fibreglass copies of antique lead troughs and terracotta urns to richly glazed Vietnamese and Provençal pots. Many of these containers are so decorative that there is a risk of 'gilding the lily' when you plant them. Generally, you should aim for a simple architectural effect rather than glorious profusion.*

Much imported terracotta is inexpensive and very decorative but not frost-proof. It can be used for summer planting but must be brought indoors for the winter. In cold areas it is best to buy terracotta which has been fired at very high temperatures to withstand frost damage. If you use saucers under pots in summer, it is vital to remove them in late autumn as even the toughest pot will crack if left standing in frozen water.

Lining decorative pots with slightly

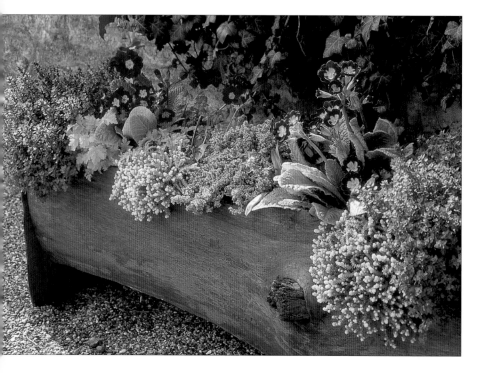

BELOW A rustic wooden trough makes an excellent home in spring for dwarf hebes, polyanthus and scillas, the latter replaced in summer and autumn with a seasonal display.

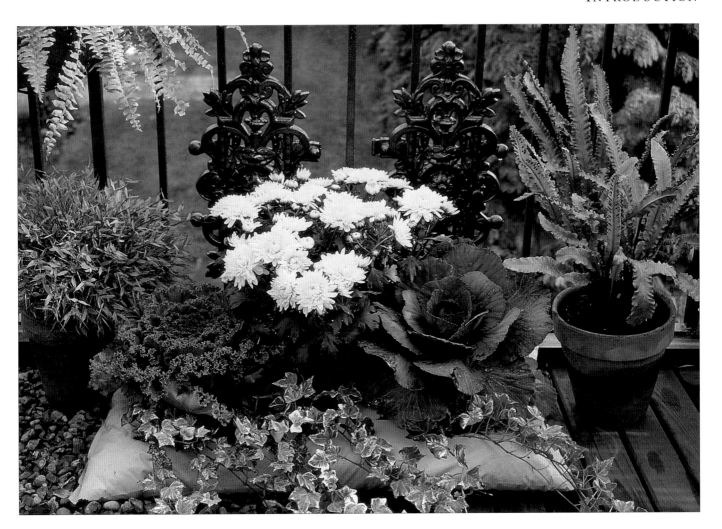

smaller plastic pots avoids having to discard spring flowers that are still looking good to get the summer planting established.

Reclamation yards are excellent sources of unusual containers, especially when you are looking for something fairly large as a focal point. They are also good places to find plinths, columns and chimney pots. Look for smaller containers in junk shops and flea markets – an old tin bath with a hole in it is useless for its original purpose but can look great planted up with spring bulbs, and a metal bottle-carrier will hold pots of flowering plants just as well as bottles.

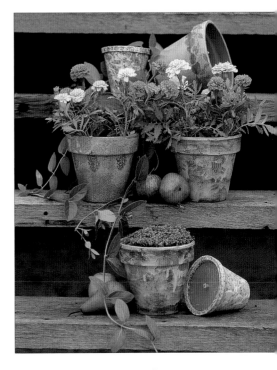

TOP *Even a growbag assumes designer status when its contents are colour coordinated.*

ABOVE *Simple terracotta pots can be painted to add interest to any planting display, as these little pots of marigolds demonstrate.*

27

CLASSIC CONTAINERS

A lushly planted classic urn is all that is needed to give a small space both drama and elegance. Whether set against a backdrop of unadorned brick or stone, or backed by a mass of climbing plants, its outline will furnish its surroundings and draw the eye. It adds instant height and structure to a garden, and a sense of the theatrical.

SOME CONTAINERS are very much secondary to the plants that grow in them but this should not be the case when using classic containers, such as stone urns. These are beautiful objects in their own right, and can even be used unplanted as sculptures during the winter. In the spring, densely planted with tulips (*Tulipa*), an urn is a dramatic focal point while luxuriant summer planting will soften its outline but still make sure that it is the centre of attention. To be best admired, the urn should be placed at eye-level on a ledge or plinth – at ground level its outline is too easily lost amid its surroundings.

The planting can take the form of eye-catching feature plants (see pages 122-3), foliage plants (see pages 124-5) or a mixture of trailing plants (see pages 126-8) that drape attractively over the rim of the container. Make sure the planting colours and textures complement the style of the pot.

When planting the urn for summer, choose a central plant that has sufficient drama of its own not to be overwhelmed by its container. It should grow to the same height as that of the urn and spread well over its sides, although more upright plants can be used in combination with trailing plants which will provide the width. It is essential to water the urns daily and to feed and dead-head the plants regularly – a compelling visual statement such as a classic urn will inevitably be a prominent focal point and neglect will be very noticeable.

PLANTING A GRAND URN

Grand containers deserve to be filled with equally grand plants. An exuberant Datura (syn. Brugmansia) spills out of this container and towers above all the other plants in the border. The rounded shape created by the various leaves and flowers is the perfect foil to the urn in which they are planted. The plants used for this display are shown below.

Datura (syn. Brugmansia)

Helichrysum   *Salvia patens 'Cambridge'*

Verbena

PLANTING A SUMMER POT

This impressive container makes a very dramatic statement among the surrounding greenery. The plants used are:

Melianthus major

Helichrysum microphyllum

Pelargonium 'Voodoo'

Salvia 'Raspberry Royale'

Argyranthemum 'Flamingo'

UNUSUAL CONTAINERS

The adventurous gardener may find the choice of pots available at most garden centres rather sedate, while the more unusual commercially available alternatives are frequently very expensive. There are, however, plenty of wonderful containers to be found in junk shops, reclamation yards and even in your own attic. Gardening is, after all, an expression of each individual's creativity and this need not be limited to your choice of plants. Quirky containers are fun, eye-catching and original.

WHEN WE BUY new containers for the garden we rightfully expect them to be in perfect condition and to prove durable. This need not be the case with unusual containers, which are frequently objects that have been discarded because they no longer fulfil their original function. They may only last two or three seasons before they finally collapse, but in the meantime you will have had the pleasure of an inexpensive container and you can enjoy a more creative form of recycling than taking your bottles to the bottle bank.

A woven basket that has lost its handle is useless for carrying things but is charming as a moss-lined container for alpine strawberries or pinks (*Dianthus*). An old black saucepan, rusted through at the bottom, is an appropriate container for otherwise invasive mint (*Mentha*) when placed next to the kitchen door, and a wooden wheelbarrow, discarded because its wheel wobbles and it can barely be lifted, becomes a decorative planter.

Just because you have never seen something used as a container before does not mean it can't do the job. Provided you create some drainage holes and there is room for a sufficient depth of soil, practically anything can become a planter. However, bear in mind that unusual does not have to mean tacky – old car tyres and lavatory pans work as containers but they seldom look decorative, so keep your aesthetic sensibilities about you when searching for something new.

TOP *An unusual sculpted animal head is adorned with ferns and grasses.*

LEFT *Disused cooking pots make ideal planters for small spring bulbs.*

RIGHT *A wheelbarrow makes a planted feature in a small courtyard when filled with small succulents.*

OPPOSITE PAGE *The open drawers of an eclectic mixture of discarded furniture create a novel form of tiered planting in a small backyard.*

FEATURE CONTAINERS

When strikingly planted, one grand, large-scale container can form the centrepiece of a small space and inspire the rest of the planting. It can even be the only significant planting in an area that otherwise consists of varied textures of hard landscaping such as stone, brick or paving that will become softened in time by moss and creeping plants. Raising the container above the level of the surrounding planting will often further increase the impact.

PROBLEM CORNERS or difficult spaces can become a positive asset in the small garden when plants and containers are imaginatively combined. Allow yourself to be inspired by other people's bright ideas and keep a notebook at hand to record particularly good plant combinations or inspired marriages of plants and containers. Planting schemes from famous gardens can be scaled down most effectively.

Even the smallest space can take one large, dramatic plant. This generally works best when the plant has architectural or textured foliage or flowers. Hostas (*Hosta*), ferns, cordylines (*Cordyline*) and New Zealand flax (*Phormium*) all have handsome foliage; lilies (*Lilium*), Angel's trumpets (*Datura*) and peonies (*Paeonia*) have glorious flowers; and the globe artichoke (*Cynara scolymus*) has serrated silver-grey foliage and magnificent, purple thistle-like flowers.

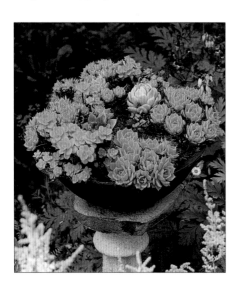

TOP LEFT *The shimmering leaves of* Helichrysum petiolare *catch the light.*

LEFT *A bowl of succulents atop a stone column makes a bold statement.*

ABOVE AND FACING PAGE *Large containers of architectural plants stand out dramatically from the surrounding greenery, as with the variegated-leaved hosta (above) and the fern (right).*

TROUGHS

Troughs are often the ideal planters for

narrow spaces, including windowsills and

balconies. An attractive view can be framed

with colourful low-growing plants while a less

decorative outlook can be masked by more abundant foliage and flowers.

When selecting your plants choose some that are fragrant so their scent will

waft through an open door or window.

TROUGHS COME in many forms, including wood, stone, terracotta and metal. Choose colours and textures of container that are appropriate for the setting. If your budget will not run to expensive containers, why not consider recycling household containers instead? The most interesting gardens often feature containers that have been adapted from their original purpose. While many of these containers have previously been used as the manufacturers intended, it is also possible to buy them new and to use them in the garden from the outset. Polystyrene wallpaper troughs fall into this second category. They are inexpensive and available from DIY stores, easy to paint and have the added benefit of being very lightweight, making them ideal for roof gardens and balconies where weight can be a serious consideration. Most of the manufacturers of these troughs have now realized that they have an alternative use in the garden and so considerately mark the base of the trough to show where drainage holes should be made.

Although lacking the inherent strength of most containers, polystyrene is actually a very plant-friendly material because it absorbs and retains warmth from the sun and therefore stimulates good root growth.

PREPARING A WALLPAPER TROUGH

1 Turn the trough upside down and use a hammer and screwdriver to pierce the drainage holes following the manufacturer's markings. If there are no markings, make eight holes in two parallel lines along the base.

2 Place the trough on a protected work surface and paint the sides and the base. Allow to dry, then paint the rim and the inside to below soil level. You can use emulsion paint, but red oxide paint gives a more durable finish.

ABOVE *Filled with summer-flowering gazanias and portulacas, this wallpaper trough has been painted terracotta, successfully disguising its origins as a wallpaper trough. Adding a few* objets trouvés, *such as these scallop shells, increases the decorative effect.*

RIGHT *Echeverias fill a long concrete trough, their flowers spilling over and softening its outlines. Daisy-like plants (Erigeron karvinskianus) also help to create a natural look.*

SMALL CONTAINERS

While small containers can go unnoticed in a large garden, they are essential components of the small garden, terrace or balcony. Here, every pot and planter should be chosen to make a positive contribution to the scene, and the plants changed seasonally for a continuous display or selected so they will look good throughout the year. For maximum impact, plant in blocks of colour instead of mixed colours, and group the pots together rather than position them individually.

IN A SMALL SPACE, containers are an important part of the architecture and furniture of the garden. They help to create the mood – strong architectural shapes, even on a small scale, will give the space formality; rustic planters convey a cottage garden atmosphere; and brightly glazed or painted pots can transform an urban yard into a corner of the Mediterranean.

A formal space needs little more than evergreen topiary softened here or there with pots of one variety of seasonal flower in a single colour. For example, a white theme might feature pansies (*Viola × wittrockiana*) in the winter, narcissi (*Narcissus*) in the spring, tobacco plants (*Nicotiana*) in the summer and cyclamen (*Cyclamen*) in the autumn. The scale can be as small as required to suit the space; it can even be small enough to display on a table-top, with home-grown compact varieties of evergreens or herbs that have been pruned to shape and small-leaved ivies (*Hedera*) trained over frames.

The less formal space is easily given a seasonal change of colour and style. Plastic pots of plants can be slipped inside your containers so there is no need to dig them up before re-planting the container. Simply remove the plastic pot and tuck it out of sight so the plant can die back naturally.

RIGHT *Dramatically coloured black grass (*Ophiopogon *'Nigrescens') is teamed with a dark* Sempervivum. Hebe *and a pale pink viola provide contrast.*

RIGHT AND FAR RIGHT
*Use of alpine, miniature
and compact varieties of
plants such as these will
ensure that the containers
are not swamped by their
contents.*

RIGHT *A bark basket, with
its evocative woodland
associations, is the perfect
complement to the lilies of
the valley (Convallaria
majalis) nestled in
their bed of moss.*

37

MINIATURE DISPLAYS

As children, many of us enjoyed creating miniature gardens. These were usually of a very temporary nature, made out of mosses, twigs and little flowers, but this should not be a form of gardening that is abandoned with maturity – it is something that can still be enjoyed by using a more sophisticated construction. A carefully chosen shallow container planted with alpine and other little plants becomes a miniature landscape full of fascinating detail which would be unnoticed if the same plants were growing at ground level.

THIS FORM of gardening is accessible to practically anyone as it only needs the tiniest of spaces – a windowsill or table-top is quite sufficient. Miniature displays can be created by planting a single container with a group of plants or by planting choice specimens in individual pots and grouping them together. Either way you will have plants that you can tend and admire up close.

When grouping plants in a single container it works best when the container used is long and shallow, so as to be in scale with the plants; this will help you to create a miniature landscape rather than just a mixed planting. Before removing the plants from the pots in which they were grown, experiment with their positions within your chosen container. Once you are happy with their relationship to one another, plant them firmly in good-quality potting compost with added slow-release fertilizer. When planting a spring, autumn or winter garden, surround the plants with moss, while a summer garden should have coarse grit or gravel around the plants. Both of these soil coverings are decorative and also help to retain moisture and prevent the compost being splashed on to the leaves and flowers during watering. Individual specimen plants will also look better than ever when given this treatment.

RIGHT *A miniature terracotta trough (shown opposite with a summer display) is filled in spring with cottage garden favourites – cowslips, primroses and violas.*

PLANTING A MINIATURE SUMMER DISPLAY

A small stone trough or wooden container makes the ideal miniature garden because it looks good when placed at eye-level on a table-top or windowsill. It requires careful composition – choose plants whose foliage and flowers complement one another, like the summer-flowering plants shown below. Alternatively, a container filled with a single type of flower, such as snowdrops (Galanthus) in the early spring or houseleeks (Sempervivum) in the summer looks very striking, or you can create a mixed planting found in the garden centre, such as rare or unusual plants that would be overlooked if planted in the borders.

PLANTS FOR THE MINIATURE SUMMER DISPLAY

Dianthus 'Nyewoods Cream'   *Drosanthemum hispidum*   *Geranium cinereum*   *Sisyrinchium bellum*

HANGING CONTAINERS

Hanging containers are an invaluable asset when gardening in a small space. While other containers use the horizontal or vertical surfaces of the garden, hanging containers create another dimension by using the airspace.

You can create mixed plantings or use a single variety flower to make a bold statement. When space is at a premium, hanging baskets can even be used to grow herbs and miniature vegetables, such as cherry tomatoes, lettuces and aubergines.

HANGING BASKETS are really miniature gardens in their own right, with the great advantage that you have more control over the position, soil conditions and plants than in most other types of gardening. They are fairly labour-intensive, because they need regular watering and feeding to ensure a long-lasting display of flowers and foliage, but hanging baskets will reward you with a concentration of colour that can be much more elusive elsewhere in your garden.

There was a time when hanging baskets were purely for summer display; filled with colourful, tender plants they brightened the garden for a few

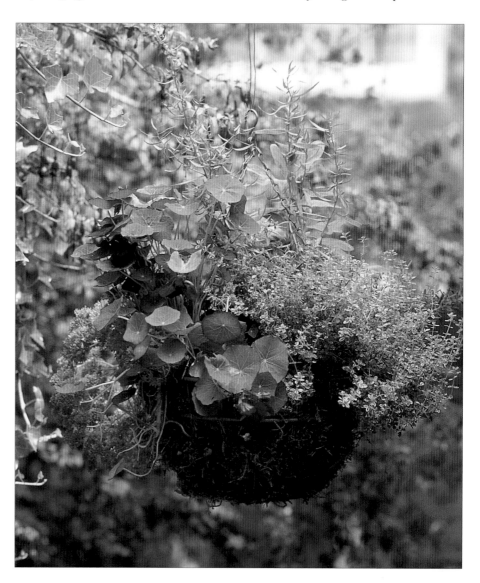

PLANTS FOR A HERBAL HANGING BASKET

Thymus

Rosmarinus

Tropaeolum

Ocimum basilicum

PLANTING A HERBAL HANGING BASKET

A densely planted basket of herbs positioned close to a kitchen doorway (above) is both attractive and useful. Regular picking will keep the herbs growing strongly and provide aromatic ingredients for your cooking. The inclusion of a plant with edible flowers, such as nasturtium (Tropaeolum), gives the basket an extra element of colour. Many colours of nasturtium are now available – choose from red, orange, yellow, apricot and peach.

PLANTING AN ALL-YEAR HANGING BASKET

We tend to think of hanging baskets as a summer feature, but when planted with evergreens and seasonal colour they can continue to look good throughout the year. A mixture of upright, decorative ferns, trailing evergreen ivy (Hedera), periwinkle (Vinca) and pansies (Viola) is the basic planting of this hanging basket (below). The small-flowered blue pansies will bloom over many months, provided that they are regularly dead-headed and occasionally cut back to encourage fresh new growth. Their colour will accentuate the blue periwinkle flowers.

PLANTS FOR THE ALL-YEAR
HANGING BASKET

Polypodium vulgare

Dryopteris erythrosora

Cyrtomium fortunei

Vinca minor

Viola × wittrockiana

months. Now, they are increasingly filled with seasonal plants for spring and autumn displays and, in milder areas or sheltered corners, hanging baskets can be used to relieve the winter gloom. Garden centres stock many suitable plants throughout the year and some even sell colour-themed selections which are ready for planting. This is often a good starting point for the beginner as the plants will have been chosen for their suitability for hanging baskets.

It is vital to have a strong bracket with good fixings for a hanging basket –

a recently watered basket filled with plants can be very heavy and could inflict serious damage were it to fall. For a colourful display it is best to locate the bracket where the basket will be in the sun for some of the day. However, if this is not possible there are plants that will flower happily in shade and when mixed with variegated foliage they can still provide a splash of colour – use violets (*Viola*), pansies (*Viola × wittrockiana*) and miniature bulbs during the cooler months and busy Lizzies (*Impatiens*) throughout the summer.

DOORWAYS & STEPS

If the truth be told, many of us are fair-weather gardeners and there are parts of the garden which we only visit when the sun shines. However, doorways and steps do not fall into this category – these are used daily, so planting should be planned accordingly.

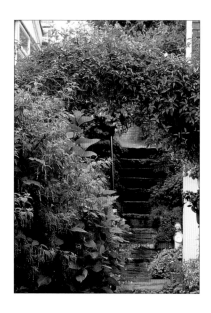

Steps make a wonderful showcase for pots of plants that are looking their best, as the flowers can be admired from many angles, while a doorway provides the perfect frame for climbers.

ABOVE *Fuchsia and clematis mingle together in a courtyard entrance. Many varieties of fuchsia, and some clematis, will do well even in partial shade.*

RIGHT *Areas with little planting space can still support an astonishing variety of plants, using climbers on walls and containers on every ledge and step.*

CLIMBING PLANTS, *hanging baskets and wall pots can be used to frame a door, and if you incorporate evergreen and hardy plants there will always be something of interest. An evergreen clematis such as C. cirrhosa will flower in mid-winter as its bronze foliage twines among the bare stems of a climbing rose; a hanging basket filled with ferns will look good in the coldest weather; and a display of ivies (Hedera) and pansies (Viola x wittrockiana) will keep a wall pot looking colourful in winter. Given the limitations of space, choose your climbing plants carefully – they should be reasonably compact, flower over a long period and have a good fragrance. Plants that might go unnoticed elsewhere disclose their charms when placed on steps. Pots of snowdrops (Galanthus) and hellebores are a delight with their delicate flowers which bloom in deepest winter. In summer, aromatic herbs and scented flowers thrive on the heat radiated by sun-drenched steps, and the fragrance they release will be particularly intense. Whatever the time of year, pots grouped around a doorway and on steps look charming, but do bear in mind that you still need to get into and out of the house!*

BELOW *A small gate, overhung by climbers on a pergola, is almost obscured by a lush planting of* Crocosmia *on the steps leading up to it.*

FACING PAGE *Restrained formality has turned a small courtyard, and the steps leading down to it, into an elegant formal garden, with clipped box balls, neat standards of bay and smart edgings of petunias.*

INFORMAL DOORWAYS

You need only read the phrase 'roses round the door' to conjure up a picture of an earthly paradise where all is beauty without and domestic harmony within. Although the reality may be more prosaic, it is undoubtedly true that plants growing around and over a doorway are nearly always decorative and a gentle pleasure for the occupants and their visitors.

CERTAIN PRACTICALITIES must be borne in mind when selecting plants to grow next to or around a doorway, especially when planting in a restricted space. Standard and topiary plants should be above or below face level, otherwise they are likely to inflict damage upon, or be damaged by, those who pass by. Lush growth is desirable around informal doorways but rampant plants can be more of an impediment than a pleasure and will need frequent pruning and tying in. Stems of tall, flowering plants should be well-supported or they are likely to be broken as they are brushed against. If you are using canes to support plants, be sure to slip protective covers over the ends to prevent visitors damaging their eyes as they stoop to admire your handiwork.

When choosing climbers, select varieties that flower for as long as possible and plant two or three different climbing plants together to lengthen the flowering season. If possible, include an evergreen or a climber that bears berries or fruit.

Scent is an important consideration when planting around a doorway. This is a place where people tend to linger and it is made more enjoyable when surrounded by fragrant plants. Herbs have aromatic foliage that smells strongest when brushed against or crushed.

LEFT *Evergreen holly and ivy provide subtle winter colour next to a painted door.*

RIGHT *Scented lilies (Lilium 'Casablanca'), one either side of a doorway, make an attractive feature.*

ABOVE *An ornamental bracket positioned alongside a doorway supports a hanging basket of cascading white and blue lobelia, Scaevola and Convolvulus sabatius. With an occasional trim and regular feeding, this basket will continue to flower well into the autumn.*

Plant the herbs in pots and in crevices in the paving surrounding a door. Choose varieties of climber that are strongly scented, and be sure to include plants that release their fragrance in the evening, such as lilies (*Lilium*) and night-scented stocks (*Matthiola*). Large-flowered tall plants such as lilies need staking (below).

When deciding on a colour scheme, the effect will be more coherent if you limit the palette. A single-colour theme will lend elegance to a doorway, no matter how informal it may be. If the door is painted, choose flowering plants and foliage to complement or contrast with the paint colour, because the door is central to the design and should not be disregarded. Unpainted or weathered wooden doors generally have a softer appearance and look good surrounded with muted colours such as soft blues, pinks and lavenders.

While the formal doorway generally relies on symmetrical and disciplined planting, this is not the case with the informal doorway – here, lack of symmetry can contribute to the charm and planting can be on many levels above, around and either side of the door. Use climbers over and around the doorway, with hanging baskets and wall-mounted pots for high-level displays. When using hanging baskets in this situation it is generally advisable to hang them to one side of the doorway rather than directly above the entrance – because they require frequent watering this can result in unwelcome drips on those who pass underneath. Plant abundantly on either side of the door using pots and planters of various sizes filled with a combination of tall and trailing plants.

STAKING LILIES

1 *Place some drainage material in the base of the pot and half-fill it with potting compost.*

2 *Add a layer of silver sand to ensure free drainage and position the bulbs evenly.*

3 *Cover with more compost. Push the stakes firmly into the compost at regular intervals.*

4 *As the plants grow, tie the foliage loosely to the stakes with soft string.*

ABOVE *Continuing the white theme used in the above picture, large pots either side of the doorway are planted with sweetly scented tobacco plants (Nicotiana) against a backdrop of mop-headed hydrangeas.*

47

FORMAL DOORWAYS

The most effective planting is planned to complement the style of its architectural setting, and there are many doorways where formal containers filled with evergreen shrubs are more appropriate to the house and more to the taste of the occupants than flower-filled planters which are labour-intensive and relatively short-lived.

WHILE SYMMETRY can be difficult to achieve in less formal settings, it is an easy way to add drama and style to formal entrances. Pots of topiary are a popular choice and, although they can be an expensive initial investment, they are very undemanding and look good throughout the year. Several alternatives to topiary are equally suitable for formal situations. Matched pairs of plants placed either side of a doorway can make a striking impression – for example, white mop-headed hydrangeas (*Hydrangea*), small mock topiary pots of

pansies (above) or grape hyacinths (*Muscari*), or more architectural foliage plants such as cordylines (*Cordyline*) and standard bays (*Laurus nobilis*).

In general when choosing plants for formal doorways, you cannot buy small plants and wait for them to grow. Instead, be guided by the size of the containers when you choose your plants – ball topiary and shrubs should be as tall and as wide as the container; pyramids should be one-and-a-half times the height of the container; and the stem and head of a standard should be at least double the height of the container. If

mature topiary is beyond your means, but you wish to achieve a similar effect, you can use wire topiary frames or planters topped with obelisks and train evergreen climbers over the frame – the frames and obelisks have a decorative architectural quality that will contribute to the formality of the doorway while the plants grow.

FACING PAGE *Grouping containers of foliage plants makes a bold statement. Use contrasts of form and texture, as here. Box (Buxus sempervirens), clipped into a ball, creates a foil for large fern and hosta leaves.*

TRAINING SHRUBS

Box (*Buxus sempervirens*) is the ideal shrub for the beginner to use for topiary. It is very easy to grow, and once established puts on a lot of dense growth each season which can be clipped into simple balls or pyramids. Initial success will inspire you to try more adventurous shapes.

ABOVE AND RIGHT *Regular clipping of new growth during the growing season is the best way to ensure a well-shaped shrub. Irregular pruning can eventually result in 'leggy' growth which spoils the dense outline of the piece of topiary.*

ABOVE *Clip pairs of box shrubs into symmetrical shapes and place either side of a doorway for a simple, elegant effect.*

Hot-coloured Baskets

Vibrantly coloured flowers seem to absorb and radiate the heat of the summer garden, and even on a dull day their intense hues will make an impact. These are jolly, extrovert flowers and used in a hanging basket they will dominate a small space like an aerial exclamation mark and set the mood for the rest of the garden. Busy Lizzies (right), petunias, nasturtiums and trailing geraniums are all good candidates for such a display.

Hot-coloured flowers are generally sun-loving and you will have no difficulty finding suitable plants for a sunny position. Ivy-leafed pelargoniums are available in brilliant cerise, magenta and dark crimson as well as more subtle shades, and they look wonderful with petunias and verbenas in bright colours. The smaller-flowered tumbling petunias are particularly good in hanging baskets and so prolific at flowering that they can be used on their own. For real drama you can mix what are conventionally thought of as clashing colours – putting scarlet, purple, orange and cerise together may seem risky, but in reality it looks fantastic provided that the rest of your garden can match such a positive statement. These strong colours work particularly well with an architectural setting as a backdrop.

For a shady garden, the pansy (*Viola × wittrockiana*) and the busy Lizzie (*Impatiens*) are perfect for hanging. Both prefer shade and a hanging basket of either flower will establish quickly and add colour in an area that usually relies on foliage plants and pale-hued flowers.

ABOVE AND RIGHT *Vibrant colours are the hallmark of busy Lizzies (*Impatiens*), which make superb hanging baskets, thriving in either partial shade or sun.*

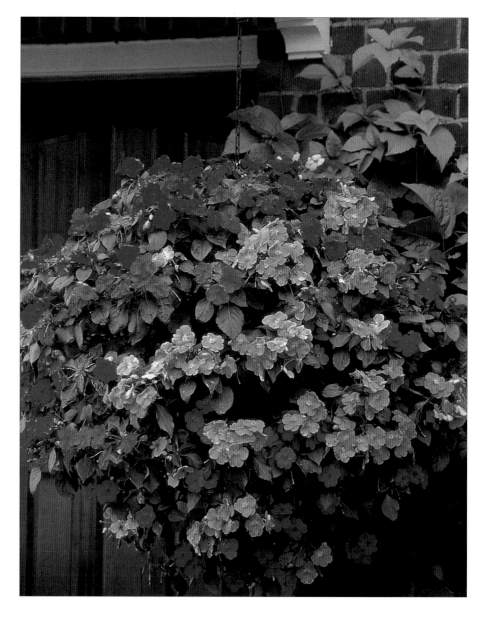

PLANTING A HANGING BASKET

1 *Line the basket with moss, partially fill with compost, add some water-retaining crystals and start to plant up.*

2 *Continue to add the plants, ensuring some are pushed through the sides of the basket, and fill with compost.*

Hanging baskets come in various sizes but they will all be much larger when fully planted, so bear this in mind when purchasing an appropriately sized container. You can buy preformed liners or you can line the basket with moss. Of the two, moss is the better option, as it provides good insulation from drying winds and retains moisture well. It also looks more natural and it is easy to push the plants through the sides of the basket to ensure a more rounded, fuller outline when fully planted.

If you include a small amount of water-retaining crystals in the compost for the basket, you can cut down on the amount of watering required. Remember when planting up the basket that the plants will spread considerably when fully grown; nevertheless, err on the generous side – nothing looks worse than a sparse hanging basket. It will take a month or so for the hanging basket to look its best. The one above was photographed two weeks after planting; the blue and silver hanging basket on page 53, photographed three weeks after. Not all plants will fill out as quickly as others. See pages 126-9 for suitable plants.

3 *Tidy up the planting, trimming off any straggling shoots with a pair of sharp scissors, to create a balanced shape.*

PLANTS FOR THE YELLOW AND RED DISPLAY
Shades of yellow and red, backed by green foliage, create a hot-coloured display using the plants shown below.

FROM LEFT TO RIGHT Sedum sieboldii, Coreopsis grandiflora, Begonia, *yellow summer pansies* (Viola sp.), *red summer pansies* (Viola sp.), Solenostemon scutellarioides, Hedera helix, *and dwarf chrysanthemum.*

TONING BASKETS

Hanging baskets are among the most colourful displays for the garden as well as the most space-saving, because they can be hung from any sturdy overhead structure. Although hanging baskets can look marvellous when they are a kaleidoscope of colour, a more sophisticated look is achieved when the baskets are colour-themed.

YOU CAN create colour contrasts or harmonies with any planting scheme, according to the situation you envisage for the baskets. They look impressive displayed as a pair either side of a doorway, but asymmetric displays also work well in limited spaces. Where there is more than one hanging basket in an area it is usually best to plant each one with the same selection of plants or they may look rather muddled. Alternatively, each basket can be planted with a single colour to create blocks of colour – this is very effective against a background of dark foliage.

Choosing colours that go well together from a range of plants with more or less the same flowering season can prove tricky, particularly when the habit of the plant is critical as well. For hanging baskets, the ideal plants have a lax habit, fairly rapid growth and a long flowering season. It is now possible to buy colour-themed collections of hanging basket plants from the garden centre and, although they are not always the most exciting selection of plants, they are a good starting point and can easily be enlivened with a few imaginative flourishes of your own.

PLANTS FOR THE PINK AND MAUVE DISPLAY
The plants below, a mixture of annuals and perennials, have been used to create the display shown above.
FROM LEFT TO RIGHT Lavender stoechas *'Papillon'*; Hedera; Helichrysum petiolare *'Aurea'*; Dianthus; Pelargonium; *New Guinea* Impatiens; Fuchsia; *and* Viola × wittrockiana.

PLANTS FOR THE BLUE AND SILVER DISPLAY

Again, a mixture of annuals and perennials (below) in toning colours has been used to create the display above, with blue pansies predominating.
FROM LEFT TO RIGHT Salvia officinalis; Hedera; Viola × wittrockiana; Salvia farinacea;
Senecio maritima; Viola × wittrockiana; Helichrysum microphyllum.

FOLIAGE STEPS

Steps are a great asset in the small garden. They mark a change of levels, which always makes a space more interesting, and provide a tiered display area that shows off plants to great advantage. Using foliage plants on steps can be as simple as allowing ivy (Hedera) to cascade down from surrounding walls, or they can be the setting for splendid architectural plants or topiary and become a focal point of the garden.

WITH FOLIAGE planting it is easy to keep steps looking interesting all year round, whatever your chosen style of gardening. Informal steps are often made from a mixture of materials – bricks, stone, tiles, slates and even wood – and there are usually crevices into which you can tuck creeping plants such as sedum, sempervivum, *Arisarum* and saxifrage that will spread and soften the whole area. This is particularly useful where space is very limited and there isn't enough room to stand pots on the steps.

In formal settings the choice of containers is critical. A miscellaneous collection of pots of varying materials is not appropriate as they will look too casual for the effect you are trying to create. Simple terracotta pots lined up on either side of the steps will be far more effective than a hotchpotch of pots and planters.

When it comes to formal planting, topiary, standards, architectural and compact evergreen shrubs all look good, but you don't have to restrict yourself to the usual box (*Buxus sempervirens*), bay (*Laurus nobilis*) and ivy (*Hedera*) – many other more unusual varieties of plants are worth considering. The star jasmine (*Trachelospermum diffusum*) is a handsome, evergreen climbing plant with glossy, green leaves that become tinged with red in winter, and it has the added bonus of small, sweetly scented white flowers in the summer. Trained on to a frame, it is a good addition to sunny steps, as are standard herbs such as rosemary (*Rosmarinus*), cotton lavender (*Santolina*) and wormwood (*Artemisia*).

For shadier positions, take inspiration from Japanese gardens. Glazed pots of compact bamboos, azaleas, ferns and rhododendrons grouped with bun moss and smooth river stones covering the soil around the plants will convey a suitably lush, green atmosphere.

In exposed positions, low-growing plants are often more appropriate. Stone bowls or troughs of sempervivums or sedums have an interesting textural quality and will tolerate a wide range of weather conditions.

If you enjoy scent, remember that there are some scented plants which also have handsome foliage. Neatly clipped artemisia (see page 56) looks good in terracotta pots and is highly aromatic. Equally aromatic is the slow-growing evergreen Christmas box (*Sarcococca*), which looks attractive planted in groups.

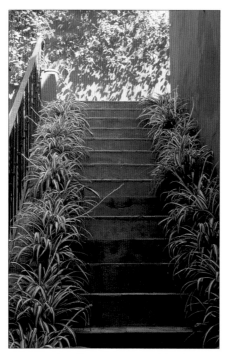

ABOVE *Small grasses or grass-like plants make a neat edging to steps.*

ABOVE *Wide steps leading to a veranda create an opportunity for a tiered display of handsome foliage plants, including box topiary (a box spiral is shown on the facing page, above) and a tender lemon tree (Citrus sp.).*

LEFT *Narrow steps can be flanked with containers of handsome foliage plants, such as agaves or yuccas.*

SCENTED STEPS

The fragrance released by plants when you brush against them is highly evocative; it can conjure up memories of childhood, recollections of other gardens, and reminders of hot summer holidays. Our sense of smell connects directly to our emotions, which is why we react with feeling to smells both pleasant and unpleasant. Scented plants growing alongside steps create a fragrant corridor that will envelop all those who pass along it.

WITHIN THE CONFINES of a small garden, terrace or balcony, fragrant plants can work their magic to maximum effect, filling the air with a scent that may be lost in a larger area. By concentrating aromatic planting on steps, alongside paths and around doorways, you will be able to enjoy the scent whenever you venture outdoors.

Provided the steps are wide enough, the most effective way to use scented plants is in containers. As with other areas in the small garden, using pots and planters allows you to move the plants around so that the star performers are to the fore while those that are past their best can be relegated to the background.

Although one generally associates scented plants with high summer, there are plants with fragrant flowers or foliage that can be appreciated throughout the year. Many herbs, such as lavender (*Lavandula*), *Santolina*, thyme (*Thymus*) and rosemary (*Rosmarinus*), retain all or at least some of their aromatic foliage during the winter when they can be placed alongside fragrant flowering shrubs such as witch hazel (*Hamamelis*), *Viburnum* and Christmas box (*Sarcococca*). These shrubs can be grown in containers and kept compact by regular pruning. From early spring onwards, line the steps with pots of scented bulbs and fragrant wallflowers (*Cheiranthus*) and include a pot of the delicious daphne. As spring advances into early summer, the choice of aromatic plants becomes ever wider as the sharp, clean scents of spring give way to the heady fragrances of summer, and the temptation to linger on the steps will become irresistible.

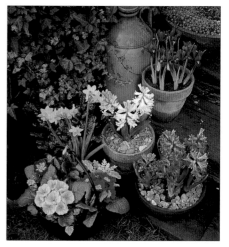

LEFT *Repeat planting on steps creates greater impact than when the planting is mixed.*

TOP *A formal pot of aromatic artemisia.*

ABOVE *Scented spring-flowering bulbs provide a tiered display on a flight of steps.*

FACING PAGE *Plants that grow happily in the Mediterranean will flourish on sunny steps.*

WALLS

Not every garden has a wall that makes a handsome architectural feature, but almost all have some form of enclosing structure which can be used to support plants. Brick or stone walls also offer the opportunity to use the tops for plant displays, with the added virtue that they deter intruders. Vertical planting

increases the available space immeasurably, so use it to greatest advantage either as a support for climbers, or by putting up trellis or shelves to display repeating groups of small plants.

ABOVE A ledge provides the opportunity for container-grown plants. Here, terracotta pots filled with herbs are displayed against a backdrop of climbing foliage.

RIGHT Colourful containers of clipped box and Muscari armeniacum are lined up in impressive formation along the tops of sturdy brick walls.

M OST GARDENERS *aspire to a walled garden but, even if that is a dream that few of us will realize, we all have gardens with at least one wall, even if it is only the external wall of our house. Any wall is an asset in a garden. In a small alleyway or on a balcony, walls are the largest planting area available, whether covered with climbers, tiered plants, wall pots or hanging baskets. On a small terrace or in a courtyard, using the walls as a vertical garden frees up precious ground space for a table and chairs or a feature such as a fountain, pond or piece of statuary.*

A brick or stone wall is a wonderful background for climbing, tumbling or trailing plants, but not all walls are made of such attractive materials – some may be in poor condition and need disguising to look their best. Faced with this type of problem, a good solution is to paint the wall in a dark colour and then cover the surface with trellis. The wall will fade unobtrusively into the background and the trellis will provide secure

BELOW Wall pots, attached to trellis, can make a colourful display that changes with the seasons. Here, Primula obconica and ferns create a splash of colour.

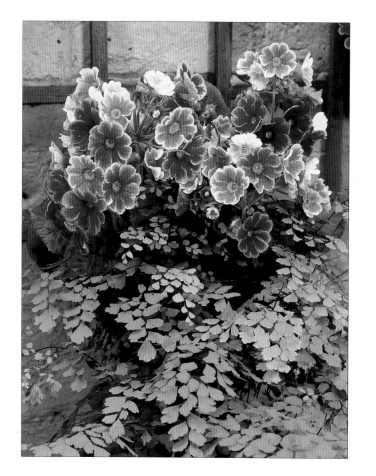

FACING PAGE (Top) A mask wall mount, capped with bright busy Lizzies, creates a focal point on a brick wall. (Below) In a shady spot beneath an old stone wall, clothed with climbing clematis and honeysuckle, a little display of corydalis, poppies and ferns amongst old terracotta pots catches the eye.

fixings for your plants. If you place containers on a high wall,

you must ensure that they will not blow down and cause

damage. To increase the height of a wall or fence, consider

attaching trellis to the top. Painted a sympathetic blue or green,

trellis looks good on its own, but will also provide the perfect

support for any twining climber, such as honeysuckle or clematis.

AURICULA THEATRE

Even in the smallest garden it is possible for plants to flower unseen. Tucked under the foliage of larger plants or overwhelmed by a vigorous neighbour, their beauty can be overlooked when they flower close to the ground. Placing decorative plants at eye-level by displaying them on shelves or other wall-mounted features, such as an old garden sieve, makes it possible to appreciate them fully when they are at their most beautiful.

AURICULA (*Primula auricula*) theatres first became popular in eighteenth-century England. Immigrant Flemish weavers would hold 'Primrose Feasts' where they would display their prize plants on black-painted shelves which would emphasize the dramatic markings of the auriculas. Fashionable society soon took up the hobby, and enthusiasts built elaborate theatres draped with black velvet with reflecting mirrors and lamplight which they filled with prize auriculas to impress their guests and cause envy among their neighbours. Although much of this was pure conceit, there was a certain practicality because many of the dramatically marked varieties of auricula need to be fully sheltered from wind and rain to keep their flowers in good condition.

Nowadays few gardeners have the space or time to devote an area of the garden to a single variety of plant that flowers for just one month in the late spring, but a small area of wall space that can be used to display plants when they are in their prime is feasible even in the smallest of gardens. The 'theatre' can be as simple as a timber shelf mounted on brackets, but if you prefer something more decorative you could make or buy a pretty, unpainted pine shelf unit and paint it with black wood

preservative before mounting it on the wall. Old terracotta pots used as sleeves for plastic pots will add an appropriate finishing touch.

Whatever form your 'theatre' takes, you will be able to use it throughout the year to display your small treasures. From the beginning of the year when

there will be snowdrops (*Galanthus*), celandines (*Chelidonium*) and crocus (*Crocus*), through the abundance of spring and summer to the rich colours of autumn cyclamen (*Cyclamen*) and heathers (*Erica, Calluna* and *Daboecia*), there will be an ever-changing tableau to admire and enjoy.

DIVIDING AURICULA PLANTS

To ensure a continuing display of healthy auricula plants it is advisable to split the plants after flowering. The young plants will quickly establish themselves and be ready to flower the following year.

1 *Gently remove the auricula plant from its pot, shake away some of the soil and carefully separate the plantlets from one another by teasing the roots apart.*

2 *Plant the young plantlets in individual pots filled with a mixture of two parts compost to one part coarse grit. Water well and stand in a cool position for the summer.*

LEFT An old shelf unit is painted black and given a new lease of life as an auricula theatre. Top row: 'Marie Creuse' and 'Walton'; second row: 'Sirius' and 'Old Mustard'; third row: 'Marie Creuse' and 'Sandwood Bay'.

ABOVE Auricula plants are very tough and do not need a great deal of attention. Originally alpine plants, they still retain their inherent vigour. Breeders have created many varieties, including this pretty blue 'Walton'.

ABOVE 'Sirius' is a variety of auricula particularly recommended to the beginner. It is very easy to grow and its stunning buff and plum flowers are produced in great abundance.

REPEATING WALL POTS

One of the advantages of a small garden is that the boundaries of a

terrace are often walls or fences which can be used for additional planting.

Just as a room benefits from decoration on the walls as well as the furniture on

the floor, so a terrace becomes much more interesting if the pots are not only sited

at ground level but also up, and on top of, walls and fences. This creates a complete

surrounding of colour and texture.

ALTHOUGH WALLS ARE ideal supports for climbing plants, they can create the perfect planting opportunity for equally striking displays of perennials and annuals. You will enhance the impact of such a display if you orchestrate a series of containers, either along the top of a wall or in pots attached to a trellis, with similar plantings, like the repeating pots of lavender on the wall top, below, or the little terracotta pots of pansies and violas beneath them. Trailing plants, such as decorative small-leaved ivies, can be used both

to soften the outline of the pots and to clamber up the wall or trellis unaided. Make sure the wall or fence is in good condition, and paint any wood with preservative at regular intervals.

Trellis makes an ideal frame for climbing plants in troughs at ground level and also provides fixing points for wall pots to create a lush effect while the climbing plants are still establishing themselves. Wall-top troughs and pots may need to be secured in place with brackets (see Garden DIY, pages 116-7) to make sure they don't become dislodged.

LEFT *Alternating troughs of lavender (Lavandula) and pots of variegated ivy (Hedera) soften this wall top and also act as a deterrent to intruders.*

RIGHT *This trellis-covered wall is softened by evergreen climbing plants and ivy (Hedera) which look good throughout the year. They are further enhanced by seasonal splashes of colour in the other wall pots, which are planted with petunias in shades of blue and purple.*

TERRACOTTA WALL POTS

Unless you own a mature garden you will probably have an area of bare wall or fence that can be greatly improved by the addition of terracotta wall pots. Even when empty these have a decorative quality, and with seasonal plantings they can be used to enliven an otherwise dull area with colour and lush foliage. You can also choose evergreen plants for a display that looks good in every season, perhaps adding a splash of colour with a flowering plant such as a pansy or viola.

I T IS ESSENTIAL to fix terracotta wall pots securely to the wall or fence because they are weighty objects. Don't be tempted to hang a pot on a convenient nail – with the addition of compost and plants, and the increased weight from watering, you will almost certainly go out one morning to find your pot reduced to a heap of shards, scattered compost and broken plants.

When planting the pot, be sure to use a compost that is specially formulated for containers, preferably with an added moisture-retaining gel – terracotta pots dry out far quicker than plastic because the water is absorbed by the clay and evaporates from its surface.

To look their best, these pots need careful planting and regular attention. Choose plants that do well in containers and bear in mind that if the wall pot is in a sunny position it will get very hot at times in the summer when the heat radiates off the surface behind it as well as shines directly on the pot. Therefore there is no point in choosing a plant that wilts in direct sunlight and likes a moist root run. If you are uncertain about which plants to select, ask the garden centre for advice or look for inspiration in other people's gardens. Your choice of colours should also take into account the colour of the wall or fence. For instance, salmon pink petunias (*Petunia*) look good against grey stone but horrible against red brick, and variegated foliage is more noticeable than ordinary green foliage when set against a dark background.

LEFT *A pleasingly weathered wall pot is planted with an unusual pink and blue display of spring flowers. Deep pink arabis, burgundy pansies (see detail top) and violet violas are complemented by the blue grape hyacinths growing beneath the pot and the stencilled flowers on the nesting box.*

PLANTING A SUMMER WALL POT

The same pot pictured in the spring display (facing page) has been used for the far more exuberant summer planting shown here. While the shape and general appearance of the pot is a feature in the spring, it is soon hidden by plenty of luxuriant growth in the summer. To keep a pot like this looking good, it is essential to feed, water and dead-head the plants regularly. When planning your planting, do remember to take into account the colour of the backdrop – what looks great against a red brick wall can look washed out and uninspiring when placed against a pale background. If you are unsure of what to choose, strong, hot colours will have an impact in most positions.

1 *Place drainage material in the bottom of the pot and half-fill with compost. Position the Felicia in the centre with a verbena on either side.*

2 *Plant the two helichrysum in front of the verbenas on either side of the pot and fill the central gap with the convolvulus. Add more compost.*

PLANTS FOR THE SUMMER WALL POT

Helichrysum petiolare 'Aurea'

Verbena 'Loveliness'

Felicia amelloides

Convolvulus sabatius

FLOWERY WALLS

A wall of colourful cascading flowers is a breathtaking sight and will make a real impact on a terrace or balcony, or in a small garden. To look good for as long as possible walls will need a careful choice of plants and more attention than other areas of the garden, but your efforts will be amply rewarded. Making greatest use of all the available space is the chief aim of any small-space gardener. Walls are no exception, and can be imaginatively utilized to create additional impact in the garden.

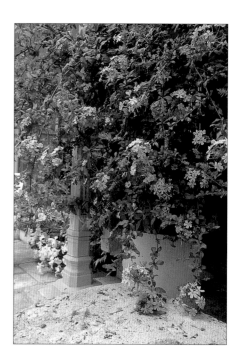

WHEN SELECTING plants for your flowery walls, look for varieties that bloom for as long as possible. However ravishing a rose may look, its value in the small garden is greatly diminished if it grows rampantly and only flowers for a month: look for roses described as 'repeat flowering' and 'compact' for a manageable, long-lasting display. When planting into the soil rather than containers, extend the flowering season by mixing climbers to flower from early spring through to autumn. The twiggy stems of early-flowering *Chaenomeles japonica* will support clematis scrambling through it to flower in the spring and summer. The passion flower (*Passiflora caerulea*) is fast-growing but worth considering for its lovely flowers, and it can be kept in check by cutting it hard back in the spring. Annual climbers such as the sweet pea (*Lathyrus odoratus*), morning glory (*Ipomoea*) and black-eyed Susan (*Thunbergia alata*) will provide additional colour through the summer.

In Spain, courtyard walls are covered from ground level to eaves with brackets holding pots of pelargoniums. This sort of repeat planting is very eye-catching and the pelargoniums thrive in the hot, dry conditions. Shelves can be used as an alternative to brackets, either wall-mounted or placed on the ground. Look for other plants that also do well in hot, dry conditions, such as begonias and nasturtiums (*Tropaeolum*), but bear in mind that these plants will still need regular feeding, watering and dead-heading in order to look their best.

TOP *Climbing plants like clematis (Clematis 'Victoria', top left) and Plumbago auriculata (top right) provide a splash of colour.*

LEFT *Vigorous climbing roses will swiftly cover a wall, filling the air with scent.*

RIGHT *Old-fashioned pelargoniums cover a wall in a traditional display.*

TOPIARY POTS

Topiary provides the perfect solution for the stylish low-maintenance garden. It also gives the garden structure even when other plants have died down. Slow-growing evergreen plants, such as box (Buxus) and bay (Laurus nobilis), are clipped into architectural shapes and planted in terracotta pots to furnish the garden with subtle but impressive style. Faster-growing climbers, such as ivy (Hedera) and clematis, can also be trained into topiary shapes over frames and will provide a similar effect in a small space for a fraction of the cost, although they will demand slightly more attention.

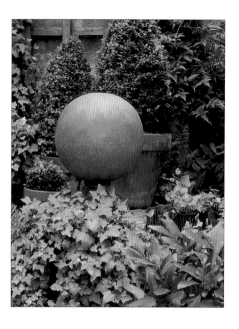

THE COMBINATION of weathered terracotta and clipped foliage is especially pleasing, and when used in a small garden they can help to create a sense of perspective and space which fussier planting would clutter. You can use terracotta and topiary to play with scale and create the illusion that your garden is a fragment of a much larger garden just out of view. Many of the great classical gardens of Europe consist almost entirely of topiary, which creates a sense of green architecture more than gardening, and the principles used in these gardens are just as applicable to a small space.

Caring for a topiary garden is very simple. Regular watering and an occasional feed with a slow-release fertilizer such as bone-meal is all that is necessary, apart from pruning to maintain the shape of the plant. If you choose slow-growing plants, such as box, the task of pruning will not be too arduous. This means you will feel more enthusiastic about doing the job. When pruning box, save some of the longer stems and, after removing the leaves from the lower half of each stem, push them into a pot of sand. Leave in a cool place to root and you will soon be growing your own topiary.

ABOVE *In an interesting reversal of the usual form, a terracotta ball rises above a base of ivy. The background of foliage throws the shape of the terracotta ball into sharp relief.*

RIGHT *Perfect symmetry isn't necessary for an eye-catching topiary display. Here, a square pot breaks the pattern as does the conical box plant which contrasts pleasingly with the other ball shapes.*

QUICK TOPIARY

Not everyone can afford to buy mature topiary, and the process of growing and training your own box or bay from a small plant can take several years. If this does not appeal, you may find the ideal solution is to use quick-growing evergreen climbers, such as ivy, which can be trained over wire frames. These frames are now available at most garden centres. Ivy is undoubtedly the easiest plant to train, and the small-leafed varieties are the most suitable for this purpose.

LEFT *A conical wire frame supports a combination of ivy and clematis. The plants look decorative even though they have barely filled out the wire frame.*

RIGHT *Ivy has been trained over a ball-shaped wire frame to create some quick topiary. The ivy can be easily clipped into shape whenever it becomes too unruly.*

MAKING AN IVY BALL

Plant the ivy in a pot which is the correct size for the frame you wish to use, separate the stems of the plant and wind them around the wires to cover as much of the frame as possible.

1 *Every couple of weeks, wind the new growth around the wires until the entire frame is well covered.*

2 *At this stage all you will need to do is to clip off any new growth, and feed and water the plant regularly to keep it in good health.*

71

CORNERS

In large gardens, corners are often neglected or used as dumping grounds for broken pots and other garden rubbish. In the small garden, where space is at a premium, a more imaginative and attractive solution is called for, and it soon becomes apparent that, far from being a problem, a corner is a positive asset. Tender plants thrive in the protection offered by a

sheltered corner; it can provide an interesting setting for an architectural plant like cordyline and it is the perfect backdrop for a plinth or a piece of garden statuary.

ABOVE *A standard tree of variegated holly* (Ilex aquifolium) *brings colour and light to a shady corner of the garden.*

RIGHT *A little pool in a corner of the garden allows you to grow a range of damp- and water-loving plants (see page 135).*

FILLING THE CORNERS of a small garden with plants can achieve a lushness and depth that might not otherwise be possible in such a small space. A corner is the ideal position for a large shrub or small tree. Choose a variety of tree that does not grow too large and preferably has a light leaf covering to avoid creating too much shade. An ornamental Malus or the winter-flowering cherry (Prunus subhirtella 'Autumnalis') are good choices because they are decorative and regular pruning will help to keep them compact. You can underplant them with bulbs or cover the area with a pattern of stones radiating out from the stem, starting 20cm (8in) away from the base, and stand pots of shade-loving plants on the stones. Hydrangeas, rhododendrons, camellias, periwinkles (Vinca), hellebores and ferns are plants that enjoy these conditions.

A paved corner that relies entirely on container planting need not be a problem. By filling the corner with a deep, square container you can create a raised bed which, when filled with good-quality soil, can be used to grow climbers to train up the walls as well as trailing plants to tumble over the sides. For a

BELOW *Majestic* Fritillaria imperialis *provides a welcome splash of colour in an otherwise dark corner.*

BOTTOM *An antique cloche, surrounded by low-growing perennials, makes a winter feature in a small corner.*

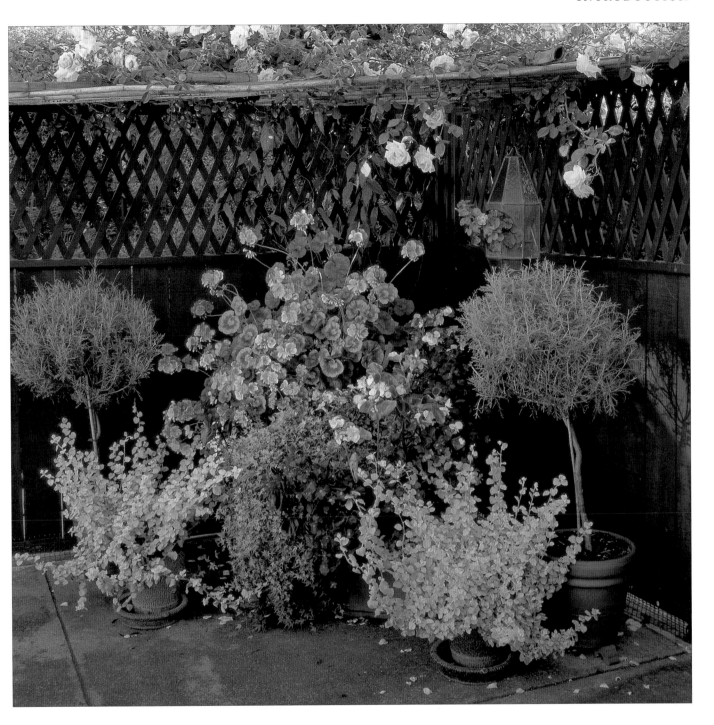

more flexible display, group pots of various sizes together in the

corner or fix a series of graduated shelves diagonally across the

corner to create a showcase for smaller plants. A corner is also

ideal for a bower of trellis with a corner seat beneath it – train

scented climbers over the bower and cluster pots of aromatic

herbs and lilies on either side to create an idyllic retreat.

ABOVE A summer display of begonias, helichrysums and geraniums in a symmetrically composed planting, flanked by twin standards, turns a corner into a feature.

FOLIAGE DISPLAYS

Often neglected, foliage plays a far more important role in gardens than most of us recognize. Although it is used as a foil for more immediately attractive flowering displays, it is well worthwhile considering foliage in its own right for small gardens in particular, and especially in shady ones where it can thrive. There are many varieties, textures and colours to choose from, and many foliage plants can be clipped into decorative topiary. Others form natural architectural shapes.

SMALL POTS of topiary – created from slow-growing evergreens such as box (*Buxus sempervirens*), bay (*Laurus nobilis*) and privet (*Ligustrum*) – and false topiary, created from quick-growing evergreen climbers like ivy (*Hedera*), will fit well into a shady corner, taking up extremely little space in the garden, while providing an interesting accent to the design. Apart from fairly minimal feeding and watering (both ivy and box cope well with drought), they will simply need clipping every now and then.

By combining topiary with architectural plants such as New Zealand flax (*Phormium*), fatsia (*Fatsia*) and spurge (*Euphorbia*), the foliage display can achieve an interesting mix of shape, colour and texture which will look good throughout the year – ideal for the lazy or absent gardener.

Hedera helix 'Glacier'

Hedera pastuchovii

ABOVE *This table-top display demonstrates the variety of colours within the green palette. Silver, gold and green mind-your-own-business (*Soleirolia soleirolii*) and a resting* Calamintha *provide a colourful display against a backdrop of ivy (*Hedera*).*

RIGHT *This shady corner is full of interesting architectural shapes, thanks to the pots of topiary ivy set against the spiky-leaved cabbage palm (*Cordyline*) and trelliswork supporting a Virginia creeper (*Parthenocissus quinquefolia*).*

PLANTING A FOLIAGE POT

1 *Place a few stones or broken shards of pot in the base of a suitable-sized container, and then part-fill with compost so that the soil level of the plant will be just below the top of the pot when it is filled with compost.*

2 *Place each of the plants in the pot, and then fill with potting compost, pressing it down well around the root balls of the plants. Water well to ensure that the roots are surrounded by soil.*

POTTED HERB GARDEN

When space is limited it is essential that the plants you choose are all-round performers, and this is certainly true of herbs. They are easy to grow in pots, gloriously aromatic and impart wonderful flavours to food. Many are evergreen and respond well to pruning into topiary shapes. They are ideal plants for small spaces.

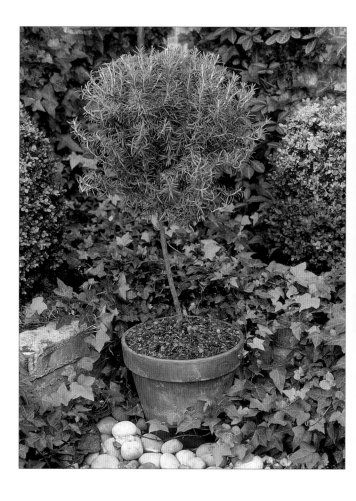

WHETHER YOUR small space is a sun-drenched courtyard, a shady balcony or something in between, there are herbs to suit all these positions. Although most herbs will tolerate most conditions, the narrow-leaved Mediterranean herbs such as rosemary (*Rosmarinus*), thyme (*Thymus*) and sage (*Salvia*) will do best if they can enjoy the sun for part of the day, while the broad-leaved herbs from cooler climates such as mint (*Mentha*), lemon balm (*Melissa officinalis*) and sorrel (*Rumex acetosa*) prefer a more shady position. Most herbs are perennials but there are some exceptions that are worth including. Basil (*Ocimum basilicum*), the king of herbs, is a tender annual that needs lots of sheltered sunshine and moist, free-draining soil. Chervil (*Anthriscus cerefolium*) is a hardy annual with delicate, aniseed-flavoured foliage that likes to grow in the shade of other herbs. Parsley (*Petroselinum crispum*) is a biennial that will grow in most places; it will last from one spring to the next but will then go to seed and have to be replaced.

TOP *A little standard rosemary (*Rosmarinus officinalis*) bush makes an ideal feature.*

ABOVE *Bay (*Laurus nobilis*) can also be trained successfully into a standard.*

FACING PAGE *Grouping herbs of varying heights together throws the different textures of the leaves into contrast.*

Mediterranean herbs like to grow in free-draining soil and will do best when transplanted into loam-based compost with added grit. Herbs are grown commercially in peat-based compost so when transplanting them it is essential to soak the compost well and gently loosen the root ball to help the roots make their way into the loam. These herbs are very tolerant of all but the most extreme cold, but they do hate to have waterlogged roots during the winter so be sure to remove any plant saucers before the cold weather arrives.

All herbs benefit from a layer of mulch on top of the compost. This helps to retain moisture during the summer, protects from extremes of cold in the winter and prevents the soil splashing on to the leaves in wet weather.

Some of the shrubby herbs, such as rosemary, myrtle and bay, are ideal for training into standards. Pinch out sideshoots as the plant grows, to leave a clear stem. When the required height is reached, pinch out the growing point; the lateral shoots will grow, creating a mop-headed plant.

SINGLE PLANTS IN A CORNER

Where space is very limited, or time in short supply, a single plant can be all that is needed to create an interesting focal point in a low-maintenance garden. By changing the plant or slightly re-arranging the surroundings you can ensure that the corner retains a freshness that continues to draw the attention. No matter what the scale of the corner in your garden you can furnish it in this way with eye-catching plants of an appropriate size.

FOR ANYONE WITH a busy life or someone who likes a nice garden but doesn't want to devote much time to pottering among the plants, a low-maintenance garden is ideal. However, although this type of garden is undemanding, it can become a bit boring. Evergreens make an excellent background but there are times when more is needed, however rampantly they climb walls and tumble over terraces. A mixture of hard surfaces also creates more interest, with stones and gravel combining well with brickwork and stone, but even when all these elements are attractively combined it can all look somewhat two-dimensional unless there is some interest in the foreground.

Planting up three or four pleasing old terracotta pots with perennial plants that will look their best at different times of year will allow you to change the look of a corner in a simple but effective way. When the plants are not in use as a focal point they can be grouped with other plants in the garden until they are ready for their moment of glory. For maximum variety choose plants that are very different in shape and colour. Hostas are wonderfully architectural with their ribbed leaves and many leaf colours, and those with variegated leaves are particularly good at bringing light to a dark corner. A plant with red or purple foliage is also a good choice as it contrasts nicely with the evergreens, and at least one plant that flowers profusely should be part of your selection. As a finishing touch, add a layer of mulch or gravel to the top of each pot.

ABOVE *The same corner with blue phlox (top); hosta (centre) and purple sage (above).*

RIGHT *Purple-leaved oxalis (right) and begonias and pansies (far right).*

OPPOSITE *Blue-leaved* Hosta sieboldiana *'Elegans' makes a handsome feature plant.*

WINDOWS

Even the smallest apartment has a windowsill which

can provide a place to grow a few plants. You can

change the display each season to make the most of

whatever is available: spring bulbs, tender annuals in

summer, evergreen foliage plants in winter. Scent

plays a part, too, particularly in summer when an

open window gives you the

chance to enjoy sweet-smelling

pinks, tobacco plants or night-

scented stocks. You can

coordinate colours in displays

and you can paint containers to enhance both the

interior or exterior of your house or apartment.

ABOVE *A summer window, surrounded by wisteria, boasts a toning display of petunias, pelargoniums and helichrysum.*

RIGHT *An eye-catching winter windowbox with a colourful display of cyclamens and ornamental cabbages.*

W HETHER YOUR HOME *is a country cottage, a formal town house or a city apartment, decorating your windowsills with plants can enhance your home and give pleasure to you and to all who pass by. Ideally, the containers you use and your choice of plants should be sympathetic to the architecture of your home. A cottage windowsill needs no more than a few terracotta pots filled with old-fashioned plants, such as scented geraniums* (Pelargonium), *pinks* (Dianthus) *and auriculas* (Primula), *while you can emphasize the formality of a town house by placing matching windowboxes on each sill and filling them with a mixture of topiary and trailing plants with added seasonal flowering plants in a single colour for a touch of brightness. In an urban apartment your windowsills may be the only garden you have, and how you choose to decorate the windowsills can be a reflection of your attitude to urban life – fashionable grasses in glazed Japanese pots for a style warrior; favourite flowers taken from friends' gardens for the reluctant urban resident; or exotic herbs and miniature vegetables for the foodie. All these and more can be grown successfully on your windowsills.*

ABOVE *By midsummer, windowbox plantings of busy Lizzies, petunias and lobelias become wonderfully full and luxuriant.*

FACING PAGE *Trailing pelargoniums in full bloom at the height of summer brighten up a plain window.*

84

HERB WINDOWBOX

You do not need even to own a garden to appreciate the pleasures of a windowsill lined with sun-loving herbs. Of all plants, aromatic herbs are particularly well-adapted to growing in a hot, dry position because this is not so different from the conditions they experienced on the rocky slopes above the Mediterranean, where so many of them had their origins. Growing herbs on a windowsill will also ensure that you can make the best possible use of the herbs because they will always be at hand whatever the weather.

WHILE MOST edible plants need to be grown in considerable quantities to supply enough food, even a small handful of freshly-picked herbs will turn a simple meal into a feast. A windowbox planted with sage (*Salvia officinalis*), lemon thyme (*Thymus × citriodorus*), rosemary (*Rosmarinus officinalis*), oregano (*Origanum*) and basil (*Ocimum basilicum*) will provide a full palette of flavours for your summer cookery.

When planting herbs as densely as this, it is advisable to choose a fairly deep container which will allow generous space for root growth and contain sufficient compost and nutrients to keep the herbs growing strongly all summer long. The addition of coarse grit to the compost will keep it free-draining, which is how most herbs prefer their soil.

One of the secrets of successful herb-growing is to keep picking the young stems regularly before they come into flower. This will ensure that the plants continue to make new growth and provide a steady supply of lush young shoots. With the exception of basil, all these herbs should survive the winter except in the coldest areas.

If you only have shady windowsills you can still grow herbs but you should choose those that do well in cooler conditions. Parsley (*Petroselinum crispum*), chervil (*Anthriscus cerefolium*), mint (*Mentha*) – a sprig of variegated mint is shown above – and sorrel (*Rumex*) are all suitable.

DISTRESSING A WINDOWBOX

There is now a very wide range of wood stains available for the garden which are preservative as well as colourful. The great advantage of these is that they are easy to apply because they are water-based, quick-drying and do not harm plants. This means that the maintenance and decoration of wooden windowboxes, tubs and planters has become much simpler. This windowbox has been given a distressed finish by first applying and rubbing down a coat of wood stain and then applying and rubbing down a coat of emulsion paint.

1 *Paint the windowbox with bright blue wood stain. When dry, rub down lightly with fine sandpaper.*

2 *Apply a light coat of emulsion paint in a terracotta shade over the blue wood stain.*

3 *When dry, give the windowbox another rub down with sandpaper so that the blue and terracotta blend together to give a gently distressed finish. The windowbox can be sealed with matt varnish or left to weather gradually.*

HERBS FOR THE DISTRESSED WINDOWBOX

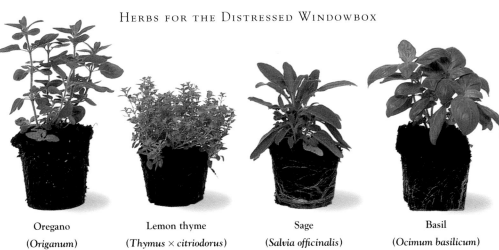

Oregano
(*Origanum*)

Lemon thyme
(*Thymus × citriodorus*)

Sage
(*Salvia officinalis*)

Basil
(*Ocimum basilicum*)

ABOVE *A windowbox filled
with the herbs (left) is a
sweetly scented addition to any
kitchen. It is also much more
convenient than having to go
into the garden whenever you
want to pick some herbs.*

PAINTED TINS

Garden centres and nurseries make fortunes selling terracotta pots and fancy planters, but it isn't always necessary to spend a great deal of money to achieve stylish results. Using a coat of bright paint, you can transform empty tin cans into attractive and functional plant holders. Be very careful to make sure that the cut edges of the tin cans have been smoothed down or covered in masking tape to avoid accidents.

ALTHOUGH THERE is undoubtedly much to inspire us in the great gardens of the world there is also inspiration to be found in simple cottage gardens with their uncontrived planting and use of 'found' materials. Old car tyres, leaky buckets and enamel saucepans are all given a second lease of life as containers for plants and now that recycling has increasingly become part of our everyday lives, there is pleasure to be gained from transforming a humble tin can into something of enduring usefulness.

In a small garden, simple planters made from tin cans are a colourful and lightweight alternative to terracotta and can be used to adorn wall spaces, windowsills and table tops. Filled with seasonal flowers which complement or contrast with the colour of the painted tins, they will provide a year-round show. The tins make charming containers for cottage garden plants and can be used to great effect on windowsills to display supermarket herbs. In this case, you do not need to provide drainage holes – instead, fill the base of the tin with a layer of gravel to prevent the herbs becoming waterlogged.

ABOVE *For a cool look, plant the tin cans with white marguerites* (Argyranthemum frutescens).

RIGHT *Plant a selection of marigolds* (Calendula) *and lobelia – the orange and purple flowers contrast vividly with the bright blue paint of the tin cans. Double-flowered marigolds (top) can be used instead.*

TRANSFORMING TIN CANS

A lick of paint will transform a tin can into an elegant container. Family-sized tin cans will hold a 10-cm (4-in) flowerpot, but for larger plants you will need catering-sized tins. Ask your local pizza parlour or Italian restaurant for their empty tinned tomatoes cans – generally, they are happy to pass them on to you.

1 Use a sturdy nail and hammer to punch drainage holes in the base of the tin cans.

2 Most tin-openers leave a smooth cut edge, but if in doubt you should cover the edges of the tins with masking tape.

3 Paint the tins with a coat of gloss paint, being careful to cover any masking tape thoroughly. Leave to dry.

SEASONAL WINDOW DISPLAY

While most garden activities are curtailed or inhibited during the colder months of the year, the great advantage of windowbox gardening is that you don't even need to venture outdoors. Simply open your window and you are ready to plant, feed and tend your mini-garden, and will enjoy an attractive and colourful display all year round.

RIGHT A spring display of dwarf narcissus and pansies in which the attractive scalloped form of the windowbox is clearly visible.

OST OF US will have enjoyed the pleasure of a summer windowbox with luxuriant flowers tumbling over the sills and delicious scents drifting indoors, but summer is the season of abundance when the windowbox must compete with many other contenders for your attention. The impact of the autumn, winter and early spring windowbox is quite different; these are times when our attention is generally focused inwards and gardening is not a daily activity, so there is a particular pleasure in looking through a window and seeing bright flowers before you notice the leafless trees, bare borders and grey skies beyond.

Some of the techniques for windowbox gardening are different in the cooler months. It is best not to use a compost with added moisture-retaining gel because this will tend to rot the roots – an ordinary, proprietary brand of potting compost used alone or mixed half-and-half with a soil-based compost will be better. Feeding is generally unnecessary and watering should only be done if the plants look very thirsty, and then only in frost-free conditions. What you can grow during the winter depends very

90

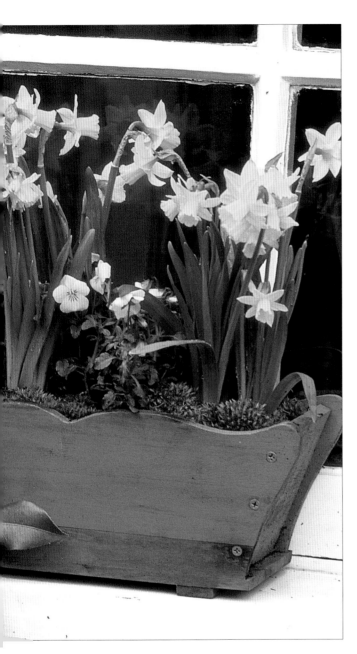

COLOUR-THEMED PLANTINGS

The following colour-themed combinations would look good at different times of the year

Winter display
Pink heathers (*Erica gracilis*) with pink cyclamens, pink winter-flowering pansies and variegated ivies.

Spring display
Muscari armeniacum, with blue pansies and polyanthus, and the same variegated ivies.

Summer display
Lobelia 'Sapphire', blue *Felicia amelloides* and deep-blue sage (*Salvia*) with thyme and ivies.

Autumn display
Purple/blue ornamental cabbages with mauve winter-flowering pansies, dwarf cypresses and ivies.

much on the area in which you live; be guided by what your garden centre recommends and accept that occasionally exceptionally cold weather will wreak havoc in such an exposed position.

Because most windowboxes are more or less at table-top level they are ideal for close-up viewing, so it is worth paying a little extra attention to detail. Choose compact varieties so they are less liable to wind damage, and look for plants that have interesting markings that will reward close inspection. Although you should not buy plants in flower in the summer, you can do so in the cooler months because the flowers last much longer at this time of year. After planting, cover the soil with moss or bark to conserve moisture.

LEFT *The window-box in its summer guise with mauve petunias and pansies, variegated coleus, and white and pink osteospermums.*

RIGHT *The winter display with cyclamens and variegated ivies.*

BALCONIES & TERRACES

If you live in a city, a balcony or terrace may be

your entire garden, but limited space does not mean

you need limit your imagination. Your terrace can be

transformed into what appears to be a fragment of a

much larger garden by using everything on a grand

scale and including mirrors to create an illusion of

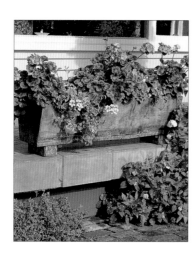

space. On a balcony,

planting on several levels

using baskets, wall pots,

shelves and columns lets

you fill your space with

colour and pay tribute to your dream garden.

ABOVE *A rustic wooden trough, filled with pink pelargoniums, links the veranda to the planting of pink busy Lizzies (Impatiens) at its edge.*

RIGHT *A handsome marble slab on classical-style pillars is the ideal place for this similarly classical formal arrangement of ivy topiary frames and a trough of salvias.*

M OST BALCONY AND *terrace gardens consist almost entirely of*

container planting. The advantage of using containers is that you

can treat the space like a stage set and move everything around

without having to uproot your favourite plants. Plan major

changes for the end of a season when you can assess the

condition of the plants and trim, feed or discard them as

necessary. This is also an opportunity to sweep up dead leaves,

dispose of any snails and slugs that you uncover and generally

give the whole area a facelift. Between the seasons, move smaller

plants around to keep the view interesting. Container plants need

regular watering and this can be very time-consuming, but there

BELOW *A balcony table in spring creates the perfect place for an informal display of flowering bulbs.*

are ways to make your task easier.

Gravel-filled saucers under the

pots will help to retain moisture

and grouping pots together cuts

down on evaporation. Plastic or

fibreglass pots need less water than

terracotta ones and are much

lighter, which can be an important consideration on a balcony. If

you don't like the look of plastic pots, slip them inside more

decorative clay containers.

ABOVE *Windowboxes can be secured to balcony rails to create attractive displays. Here one is planted with dwarf tulip 'Plaisir', saxifrages and violas.*

If you have to carry water from an indoor tap, make the effort

to fill the watering can once more when you have finished – you

can then use it on flagging plants in between your regular

watering sessions. A balcony or terrace with an outside tap can

make use of one of the automatic drip-feed watering systems

which are available from garden centres. A microchip-controlled

timer is fitted to the tap and water is fed to each plant through a

network of fine tubes. It sounds more complicated than it is, and

once set up will free you from the task of watering. All plants

grown in containers will benefit from a mulch of compost, which

retains moisture as well as provides extra nutrients.

ABOVE *On a curved terrace with wide walls, the planting follows the line of the architecture, with a seasonally changing display dominated, in spring, by containers of colourful tulips.*

95

Raised Pots

For maximum impact and variety in a small area it is essential to use the available vertical space wherever possible – not just on walls, but on the terrace and in any borders. Raising some pots above others creates a bank of colour rather than a flat plane and allows the plants to be admired individually rather than en masse.

Although pots come in many shapes and sizes, big pots are not always practical or affordable on a terrace or balcony, and without a variation in size the pots can look rather uninspired unless they are arranged at different levels. At its simplest this can be done by placing one pot on another empty, upturned pot – this can be a useful function for a cracked or damaged pot.

Old chimney pots are a very attractive and reasonably inexpensive way to raise pots and can be bought in junk shops, reclamation yards and some garden centres. Invest in a few of varying heights and they will be in constant use as plinths for raised pots. The ornate ones can be very beautiful and very expensive, but are more suitable as a focal point. The simple elegance of plain pots makes them better plinths. Topped with a terracotta or ceramic saucer they will provide a stable base for a plant.

Metal stands have a simple, architectural beauty that is suitable for a formal area with topiary and evergreen planting. Although quite expensive to buy, they are a real asset to this style of gardening. If you can't find any at garden centres, a blacksmith may be prepared to make them for you. An old-fashioned metal washstand is a ready-made alternative that would look wonderful in a more informal setting.

On the terrace or balcony where every inch of space is precious, the

positioning of a plinth against tall growing plants can give you an extra area of display between ground level and the flowers. Once you start 'layering' the plants in this way you will realize the potential to add greater substance and interest to your gardening.

For those with a taste for the classical, pillars and columns make wonderful raised plant stands. They can be topped with large urns of handsome feature plants or softer displays of trailing plants, depending on the situation and the effect you want to create. If you do

not have the budget for classical stone or marble pillars, try paint-effecting more humble plastic or fibreglass replicas. Seen from a distance, they can look deceptively like the real thing.

Whatever you use to raise the height of the planting, you instantly create a 3-D effect, giving the space a far greater depth than it would otherwise have, and increasing the apparent dimensions of the area. With clever use of raised containers, an almost jungle-like planting can deceive the eye into believing the garden is without boundaries.

Above *Chimney pots make an attractive and effective way of raising plants, creating a tiered planting of wallflowers, daffodils, euphorbia, dicentra and forget-me-nots.*

Left and top left *Metal pot stands create an opportunity to raise plants off the balcony or terrace floor. Trailing ivies are ideal for this situation.*

ABOVE *Tiered planting at the edge of a terrace, with metal pot stands and a rustic cane wigwam, helps to mark the division between terrace and garden. Raising small flowering bulbs, like tulips, to eye level increases their impact.*

LEFT *A cherub holds aloft a basket of double-flowered primroses on a terrace wall.*

HOT COLOURS

Until fairly recently it was fashionable in gardening to keep the palette restricted and to concentrate on cool, soft colours. Pretty as they are, they don't appeal to the more extrovert gardeners who like to make an impact with their plants and find the hot colours much more appealing. Fortunately for them, in the same way that many of us are now using much stronger colours in our homes and manufacturers are meeting that need, so growers are also beginning to expand their range of vibrantly colourful plants to please even the most boldly extrovert gardener.

B ALCONIES OR TERRACES are very restrictive areas in which to make a garden, where subtle planting can quickly become somewhat boring. Rather like pleasant but un-demanding wallpaper, it is appreciated when first seen but soon goes unnoticed. Hot colours grab the attention and cannot be ignored, especially when used in a small area. At its simplest you can use a single colour, even a single variety of plant massed for impact – little can rival the bright red of the geranium

RIGHT *A vibrant display of azaleas and pelargoniums, on a low table and chair, provide a splash of strong colour on a balcony.*

(*Pelargonium*) when it is in full bloom. But if even this is too subtle for you, choose the hot colours of India – orange marigolds (*Calendula officinalis*), purple heliotrope (*Heliotropium*), lime green

tobacco plants (*Nicotiana*), magenta petunias (*Petunia*), shocking pink ver-benas (*Verbena*) and scarlet geraniums. Planted separately in blocks of colour, or massed together in a glorious hotch-potch, these plants will vibrate with colour and may even cause more deli-cate souls to wince. To maintain the plants in tip-top condition it is essential to water them daily, and a regular liquid feed will help to keep the flowers and foliage vibrant. Dead-head as often as you have time and cut back any stems which become leggy to encourage the growth of new foliage and flowers. With this sort of care your balcony or terrace will remain colourful from early summer right through to the autumn.

FACING PAGE *A stone ledge creates a planting place for bright red pelargoniums.*

RIGHT *Clashing hot colours – of scarlet pelargoniums and brilliant blue lobelia, backed with hebes, provide an eye-catching display in this little alcove behind a balcony.*

EDIBLE DISPLAYS

Nothing ever tastes quite as good as home-grown food and, although the

small garden is unlikely to provide enough space for anyone other than the

dedicated enthusiast to grow serious amounts

of produce, it does add an extra, very

enjoyable dimension to gardening.

Many edible plants can be

grown successfully in containers

but it is sensible to stick to the more

decorative varieties of vegetable which

will blend attractively with the rest of the

plants in the garden.

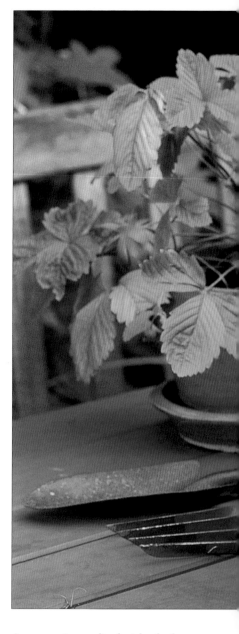

THESE DAYS, garden centres have realized that many gardeners do not have the time, space or inclination to grow fruit and vegetable plants from seed. As a result, they now stock an ever-increasing range of compact varieties of plants ready for potting up, from tomatoes (*Lycopersicon esculentum*), aubergines (*Solanum melongena*) and chillies (*Capsicum annuum*) to miniature fruit trees, all of which will perform well in pots. Look for the healthiest plants with strong stems and deep green colouring – lanky, pale plants which have been starved of food or water at this early stage will never crop well.

Try to be realistic in your choice of plants, even if you are sorely tempted by all the varieties on offer. If your garden is in more or less permanent shade, you will never be able to grow tomatoes successfully, while alpine strawberries (*Fragaria vesca*) prefer shady corners to bright sunlight. As with all gardening, growing the right plant in the right place is ultimately far more rewarding than fighting the odds.

Edible plants are 'gross feeders', which means they will need plenty of food incorporated into the compost and regular liquid feeds throughout the growing season. A layer of composted manure in the base of the pot will provide a rich source of nourishment for mature plants, and pelleted chicken manure added to the compost at the time of planting will ensure strong growth. If you add to this a weekly dose of a multipurpose liquid feed, you will be certain to produce bumper crops.

ABOVE *A moss-lined wicker basket provides the ideal growing environment for alpine strawberries and makes a particularly attractive container for these pretty plants. Placed on a shady garden table, it is an eye-catching centrepiece.*

Pests find edible plants just as delicious as we do, so you will need to be vigilant. Top of the hit-list are slugs and snails, which can chomp their way through ripening fruit and vegetables at an alarming rate.

Slug pellets are an effective deterrent to these pests, and a wide band of petroleum jelly smeared around the pot, just below the rim, will also halt slugs in their tracks. Positioning any pots on sharp gravel is another effective slug deterrent.

STRAWBERRY BASKET

A basket planted up with alpine strawberries is easy to prepare and looks extremely decorative.

1 Line the wicker basket with a generous layer of sphagnum moss to help retain moisture and prevent the compost trickling out.

2 Fill the basket with compost and plant the strawberry plants firmly so that the compost is level with the base of the stems. Water well.

ABOVE Some varieties of cherry tomato are ideal for growing in pots. The bite-sized fruit is both decorative and sweetly flavoured.

RIGHT If your tomato plants crop abundantly, their stems will need support. Here, each stem has been tied to supporting canes, topped off with tiny terracotta pots.

POOL IN A POT

A pool is a desirable and attractive feature in any garden but it can also be dauntingly expensive to install when you take into account the cost of providing a water supply and power to the garden. This pool in a pot does away with the need for both these amenities, creating an instant pool for decorative water plants and even small fish.

IN THE COURTYARD gardens of China, beautiful glazed pots raised on plinths and planted with prize waterlilies (*Nymphaea*) are often a central feature. They allow you to truly admire the porcelain perfection of the blooms and, perhaps surprisingly, provide ideal conditions for the plants.

Waterlilies flower best when growing in deep, still water in full sun and, when given these conditions, will send up a succession of flowers over many months. During the first year the plant will be establishing itself and may not flower, so the addition of some marginal water plants will add interest to the pool. Unlike waterlilies, marginal plants do not like to be planted deep, preferring to have their roots in the water and their leaves in the air. By forming a ledge on one side of the pot you can create an ideal habitat for these plants. Once planted and filled with water, the pot will quickly create a balanced environment and the only care it will require is an occasional top-up with the hose and the removal of blanket weed, the algae which forms in the presence of light. The easiest way to do this is to poke a garden cane into the centre of the mass of algae and twist it so the weed wraps itself around the cane and can be removed.

Warning This pool is not recommended in a garden used by small children. The safe alternative is a pot filled with river stones and marginal plants growing among the stones.

OPPOSITE *This pool provides a tranquil focal point in a small courtyard and needs little attention other than an occasional top-up with water.*

PREPARING A POOL IN A POT

For your pool you will require a large, glazed, frost-proof pot. The glaze is essential or the water will quickly evaporate through the terracotta. Fortunately, many of these pots are now imported from China and other Asian countries and are relatively inexpensive. Most large pots will have drainage holes in the base, but these are easily sealed with epoxy putty which is available from plumbers' merchants and also from art suppliers. Follow the manufacturer's instructions for use.

1 *Once the drainage holes are sealed, cover the base of the pot with a layer of washed stones. Any soil that settles in the base of the pot will remain undisturbed under the stones.*

2 *Plant the waterlily in an aquatic basket lined with hessian and filled with a specially formulated aquatic compost. All of these will be available when you buy the waterlily.*

3 *Place the lily basket to one side in the base of the pot. When it is in position, cover the surface of the compost surrounding the lily with more stones.*

4 *Move the pot to its chosen position in the garden. Use a couple of bricks or large stones to create a ledge inside the pot next to the lily basket and position your marginal plants. Gently fill the pot with water using a hose. Allow it to overflow to remove any debris from the surface. The pool will be cloudy for a few days until it settles down.*

GARDENING BASICS

You need very little gardening knowledge to create

successful plantings for small spaces: there are a wide

range of container-grown plants you can buy and,

provided you follow the instructions on the labels,

they should be easy to maintain. If you wish to save

yourself money, it pays to have some basic

information about choosing

plants and keeping them in good

condition, and perhaps, even

more importantly, which plants

you can raise yourself from seed

or cuttings.

ABOVE *Simple containers can be painted to give them a more attractive appearance. This little metal pot has been given a verdigris finish.*

RIGHT *A dedicated work space makes simple garden tasks easier to perform, ideally with storage under or above for equipment and containers.*

TOOLS & CONTAINERS

The basic tools you will need from the outset are shown below, and you can add to these as your experience grows, including specialized equipment if, for example, you wish to grow plants from seed and decide that a propagation unit is worthwhile. Containers are available in all sizes and materials, a range of which is shown right.

TOOLS

Try to find a proper place to keep your equipment, preferably somewhere dry and airy so that the tools will not get damp and rust, and with a work bench where you can carry out simple gardening tasks. A garden notebook is invaluable. If you can teach yourself to write down what you have bought, and where you put it, you will save yourself many months of heartache wondering what happened to the crocuses, or where you put the cyclamen corms!

Basic Cultivating Tools

There are four essential items for a basic tool kit: a garden trowel; a hand fork; a pair of secateurs; and a knife.

Secateurs

Knife

Trowel

Hand fork

Sieve

Seed trays

Preservative

Paintbrush

Fork

Hose (not essential but very useful)

Canes and ties for staking

Fine rose

Watering can

Pest Control

Insecticidal sprays can be used to control flying insects; slug pellets destroy slugs and snails.

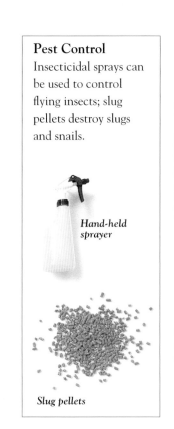

Hand-held sprayer

Slug pellets

TYPES OF CONTAINER

Containers are made from many materials, some being more expensive than others, so much depends on what you can afford and the purpose and position of the container. If you wish to create a focal point with an urn on a pedestal, for example, you may want to splurge on a quality stone or terracotta container but if you want to create an informal windowsill display, you could simply recycle household tin cans, painting them a strong colour (see below).

Terracotta ▲

One of the oldest and most traditional materials, terracotta weathers attractively, is not too expensive and suits most kinds of planting. It is quite heavy, can shatter in freezing conditions and breaks easily if tipped over.

Natural stone ▲

Durable and permanent, stone can be carved into handsome shapes. It is expensive, as well as extremely heavy.

Wire ▶

Containers of galvanized wire add a baroque touch to the garden. They are light and attractive.

▲ Plastic and fibreglass

Lightweight, durable and portable, these materials are unattractive to look at, but can be hand-painted and distressed to give a much more natural appearance.

◀ Wood

Softwood is relatively cheap but needs preserving and painting or it will rot very quickly. It is quite heavy, so should be used with care on balconies and roof terraces where the additional weight may be a problem.

Cement ▲

Although much cheaper than natural stone, cement does not have the same natural beauty. It can, however, be moulded into various shapes.

LEFT Former catering-size tomato tins have been painted bright blue and filled with colourful summer flowers.

GETTING STARTED

Before you stock your garden with plants, check that you have

at least the basic equipment needed to maintain your

garden properly. Make sure that any

containers for the plants look attractive –

they are, after all, a major part of the display

in a small space.

Y OU CAN BUY almost any plant you fancy these days ready to plant out in its own container. What determines the cost of the plant is its size – the longer it has been looked after in the nursery, the more expensive it will be. You will have to balance out the relative merits and disadvantages of each. You will get more young plants for your money, and they will establish themselves well and quickly, but they will take longer to fill the space allotted for them. Mature plants will do this more successfully, but will be slower to establish themselves and will cost you a great deal more. Plants can be bought from mail-order catalogues, direct from specialist suppliers and nurseries, or from

garden centres. Much depends on where you are living, and the kind of plants you wish to purchase. Garden centres usually carry a good range of popular perennials, shrubs and trees but specialist growers tend to stock more unusual species and varieties of plant, which may be of greater interest if you wish to develop a collection of one particular type of plant, for example. Some garden centres look after their plants better than others and the signs of a well-run plant nursery include clear labelling, weed-free, moist compost and no obvious symptoms of diseases in the plants themselves. You can also grow your own plants from seed, or from bulbs or cuttings (see pages 112-3).

Plant Size

The larger the plant, the more expensive it will be, but the quicker it will fill the available space. Use small plants for group plantings, and buy large specimens for feature spots.

Immature
Skimmia japonica

Mature
Skimmia japonica

RULES FOR CHOOSING PLANTS

• Check that the plant is not crowded in its container.
• Avoid plants where the compost at the top of the pot is weedy and mossy. The plant has been neglected.
• Pick a plant with a well-formed shape – no long, straggly shoots.
• Ensure the leaves are strong and healthy – check the undersides for signs of disease, eg mildew or whitefly.
• Avoid plants in full flower, as they stand up less well to transportation.
• If the plant looks at all out of sorts, check that its roots are not growing out through the holes in the base of the container. If they are, the plant is probably pot-bound; that is, it has grown too big for its pot.

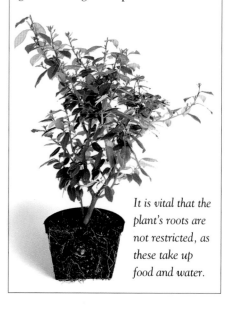

It is vital that the plant's roots are not restricted, as these take up food and water.

Composts

If you garden in a city on a window-box, balcony or roof terrace, you will need enough compost (a mixture of soil and nutrients and minerals) to fill any containers you wish to plant up. The larger the bag, the cheaper, but large bags are very difficult to handle, particularly up flights of stairs, so you may find it more practical to opt for more, smaller bags.

You will need at least two kinds of compost: one for general planting and another for propagating plants (the former being a richer mixture). You can also get specially prepared growing medium for specific types of plant: for example, rhododendrons and camellias need acid soil, and require a specially acid compost mix. Peat-free composts are considered more environmentally friendly than those which contain peat.

Container Plants

These days most plant purchases are of container-grown plants that you simply remove from their plastic pot and repot into your own container. Plants are supplied in other forms, most notably trees which are often mailed to you as bare-root specimens. Being woody and fairly tough, they will survive for a short time without a growing medium around their roots.

A container-grown palm comes in its own plastic pot, from which it must be removed and planted up in a larger pot or in the ground.

When trees and shrubs are supplied as bare-root plants, without a pot, their roots need a good soaking in a bucket of water before planting.

Planting Up

How you plant up any plant depends, to a large extent, on what kind of plant it is, and what sort of root system it has. As an idiot's guide, the roots must be covered with soil and the stem exposed to the elements. In general any container must be about 10 cm (4 in) larger than the plant in diameter. If it is bigger or smaller than that, the plant will not establish so readily. Any planting hole you make in a bed must be large enough for the plant's roots to be able to spread out properly. Repotting is really the same exercise but involves transferring the plant to a larger pot with new compost – a task carried out for most plants every couple of years when the plant will have outgrown its existing pot. If the roots start to come out of the base of the pot, you should repot the plant anyway. Do not choose a pot which is much larger than the original, as this may cause root problems. Basically, you need a new pot that is just big enough for a layer of new compost to fit around the existing root ball. Before transplanting, let the plant dry out slightly, so that the root ball slides out of the old pot easily and is not damaged in the process.

Bulbs

Bulbs are generally planted several months before they flower, so spring-flowering bulbs are normally planted in early and mid-autumn. Summer-flowering bulbs, such as the big regale lilies, are usually planted in early spring. The depth at which they are planted depends on the size of the bulb, but as a rule, plant bulbs at twice the depth of the bulb itself. Once flowering is over, move the container of bulbs to a more out of the way place, and keep the pot watered to provide food for next year's supply of flowers.

1 *Hold the plant by the stem, turn the pot upside down and ease the plant from its old pot. Fill the new pot with a drainage layer and some fresh compost.*

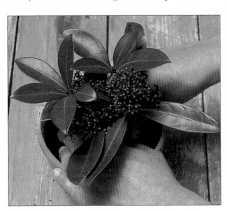

2 *Carefully insert the plant into its new pot, filling any spaces with fresh compost. Firm it in gently, then water the plant and leave to drain.*

Bulbs such as lilies produce scales that can be separated from the parent in autumn. Seal these in a plastic bag with peat and fungicide and leave in the dark for 12-14 weeks. Tiny white bulblets will form at the base of each scale, which can then be potted.

FEEDING & WATERING

Regular feeding and watering are essential to the wellbeing of any plant, but especially so for plants in containers, which can dry out and lose nutrients very quickly. To keep plants strong and healthy, there are various forms of fertilizer available which can be added to the compost to release nutrients gradually throughout the growing season, or given as a quick boost. Water should be applied frequently, bearing in mind that little and often is far better than an occasional drowning.

FEEDING

Plants will not survive very long in limited growing conditions without regular applications of fertilizer, which these days comes in a variety of forms.

Slow-release food granules can be added to the compost at planting time and will release nutrients gradually and regularly throughout the growing season. They depend on moisture to work, so ensure the compost does not dry out.

Liquid feeds are normally given weekly in the growing season. They are diluted with water according to the manufacturer's instructions, and then watered on to the compost. Most liquid feeds are multi-purpose, but you can also buy or make up specialized feeds. For example, certain formulas can give a quick boost to plants – such as to promote flowering or fruiting.

Dry fertilizer can be added to the compost at the time of planting to provide long term nutrition, or added to a border or bed after planting, taking care that it does not touch flower stems. Rain or watering will then soak the fertilizer into the compost.

Using Dry Fertilizers

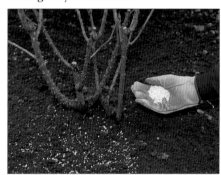

Sprinkle dry fertilizer evenly over the soil and then mix into the top layer with a fork or trowel. If the soil is dry, water after applying the fertilizer as this will help to dissolve it and wash it down towards the roots.

WATERING

Containers, in particular, dry out very fast and the chief labour in any small garden well-furnished with containers or hanging baskets is that of regular watering. In hot weather, hanging baskets may need watering twice a day. Try not to water in full sunlight, as water splashed directly onto leaves in hot sun will cause scorching.

1 Make a few small holes with a pencil around the rim of the pot to provide a conduit for the water so it reaches the roots.

Using Liquid Fertilizers

1 Dilute liquid fertilizers with water according to the manufacturer's instructions, and mix thoroughly to reduce the chance of damaging the plants.

2 Apply the fertilizer directly to the soil around the base of the plant, or as a foliar feed. Either way, nutrients will reach the plant very quickly.

2 Give an adequate quantity of water to each plant, so that the compost at the base is as moist as the compost on the surface.

Reviving a Wilted Plant

Smaller quantities of water at regular intervals are better for plants than infrequent soakings, which simply raise their stress levels, making them more prone to disease. If a plant has wilted, you may be able to revive it by placing it in a bucket of water for 10 minutes. When bubbles cease to rise to the surface, the compost is soaked.

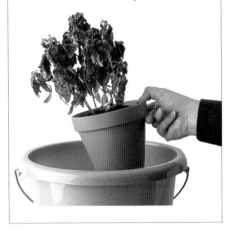

Holiday Watering

When you go away, you will need to make provision for your plants to be watered. For short-term holiday care, wick watering or capillary matting feeds water to plants via the wick or matting material from a reservoir. To help reduce evaporation in the height of summer, stand containers together on a tray of pebbles. Small plants, in particular, will benefit from this and will draw up moisture from the tray, by capillary action. In very hot weather, water the terrace or patio as well – the wet stone will help to cool down the area, reducing evaporation from containers.

ABOVE *When you go away, stand pot plants on a tray of pebbles in water. Take hanging baskets down (right), stand them on buckets in shady positions and water well. Ask a friend to water about twice a week.*

RIGHT *Hanging baskets and wall pots can be watered more easily using a hose with a cane attached to the last metre length of the hose to create a 'rigid' spout.*

Watering Hanging Baskets

Hanging baskets require copious amounts of water in summer. Being exposed to the elements on all sides, with only a thin protective covering of moss or liner for the compost, they dry out extremely quickly.

Hanging baskets can be suspended on a pulley system for ease of watering. If not, you need to construct a spout for a hose (right). It certainly cuts down on watering time if you include water-retaining gel or crystals in the compost before you plant.

RIGHT *Scattering water-retaining crystals in the compost of a hanging basket will ensure the plants do not dry out rapidly.*

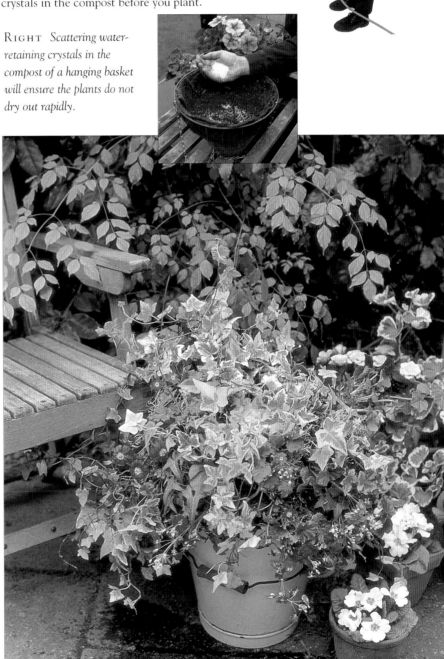

PROPAGATING

Plants can be propagated (increased) in various ways,

the simplest methods being from seed or from parts cut

off the plant (termed cuttings) which are then inserted

directly into compost so that roots form on the cut

base, creating a new plant.

GROWING FROM SEED

This method is ideal for colourful annuals, where quite a few are needed, but not worth the bother for just a couple of plants. The majority of seed packets contain hundreds of seeds and it is hardly economical in this case. Many seeds need fairly warm conditions to germinate, and once planted, are usually put in a light, warm (but not hot or sunny) place to germinate (sprout). They will not do so without an adequate supply of moisture, the amount of which needs to be carefully regulated. A plastic bag over a watered seed tray will usually provide ideal germination conditions. Once the seedlings are large enough to handle, they can then be transplanted into small individual pots, and potted on again when they are large enough to be put outside.

Collecting Seed

Choose the strongest, healthiest plants from which to collect seed, as this will ensure the best possible chance of successful propagation. Poor plants provide inferior material, and their seeds are much less likely to grow into robust new plants. Timing is also vital when collecting seeds – if you gather them too early they will not germinate, too late and the seeds will already have been dispersed.

Thoroughly dry seedheads can be hung up in a plastic bag to collect seeds.

1 *Prepare a tray of fine seed compost. Sieve the compost if necessary to remove lumps. Moisten it thoroughly.*

2 *Sow the seed at the required depth – the finer the seed the shallower the depth. For fine seed, sow in a long drill. For larger seeds (such as sweet peas), sow individually.*

3 *Water with a fine rose on the watering can. Cover with polythene and leave in a light, warm, but not hot, place until germination takes place.*

Sowing large seeds
Leaving space between the top of the compost and the pot rim, sow seeds on the surface. If the seed needs darkness to germinate, cover with a layer of compost. Water the pot from below and cover it with a piece of glass.

Seedheads of poppies, shaken onto brown paper, for collection and future use.

Sowing Seed Successfully

• Use a good quality compost.

• Use clean pots and trays.

• Remember that seeds need an initial period of darkness.

• Once germinated, seeds must have light. Turn tray around regularly to ensure an even distribution.

• Seed composts contain only enough nutrients for 6 weeks, so pot on after that.

• Seedlings must not dry out. Regular gentle watering works best.

• Thin out ruthlessly to ensure seedlings are sturdy. Plant 25 per cent more seeds than you need to account for fatalities.

• Harden off seedlings grown indoors before planting outside by exposing them to outdoor conditions in daylight for 10 days or so.

▲ *Putting seeds or cuttings in a heated propagator speeds up rooting and germinating.*

A cold frame is used ▶ *to gradually acclimatize seedlings to the outdoor conditions before planting them out.*

GROWING FROM CUTTINGS

One advantage of growing plants from cuttings, as opposed to seed, is that you know exactly what plant you will get. Generally, shrubs are grown from cuttings and annuals and most perennials from seed.

Cuttings can be taken from all parts of the plant – stems, shoots, buds, leaves and even roots – and the method differs according to which part you are using. The most commonly used type of cutting is known as the softwood cutting (shown right) which is taken from a young shoot in summer. It is relatively easy to persuade a softwood cutting to root, but some plants will root more readily than others. Good candidates for this purpose are box (*Buxus sempervirens*) and pelargoniums. Cuttings are usually taken in early or midsummer from a non-flowering shoot and will be ready to transfer into individual pots in the autumn. To take cuttings you will need a 15-cm (6-in) diameter pot, filled with cuttings compost, and a sharp knife. Hormone rooting powder can be applied to the base of the cutting to encourage rooting. It is important to use the right mixture of compost for cuttings. Usually a mixture of three parts sharp sand and one part compost is used, as it gives the necessary drainage for the plant, which in turn prevents rotting. Cuttings must be kept moist in good light but out of direct sun.

1 *Cut the shoot (in this case from a pelargonium) from the main stem of the plant, just below a leaf node, using a sharp knife.*

2 *Remove the bottom pair of leaves, clearing the lower half of the stem so it is able to be inserted into the compost.*

3 *Dip the base of the cutting in hormone rooting powder. With a pencil or dibber, make a small hole in the compost to take the cutting. Insert the cutting.*

4 *Firm soil around the cutting, water well and keep the compost moist until the new plant starts to grow. Place a clear plastic bag over the pot to form a mini greenhouse.*

MAINTAINING YOUR PLANTS

Your plants will need a certain amount of care to look good at all times. The most important tasks, apart from feeding and watering (see pages 110-1), are to stake and support them properly, and to remove any dead or dying flowers, as well as straggly growth or dying or damaged stems. Check regularly for pests and diseases, as all plant problems are most easily dealt with early on.

STAKING

Many plants, particulary soft-stemmed herbaceous perennials, require some kind of additional support to look good. There are many ways to create efficient and attractive staking systems for plants, and proprietary stakes can be bought at garden centres (see below). Be careful, when tying plant stems to a stake, not to twist the tie so tight that it damages the stem. Softer, wider ties are better than string, which can cut through weak stems.

Forms of Staking

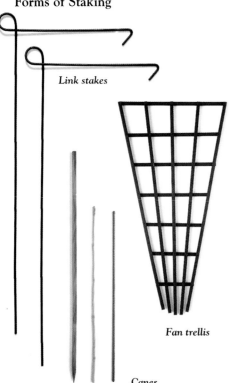

Link stakes

Fan trellis

Canes

Supporting Plants

With container plants, or plants in small gardens, any stakes should be made as invisible as possible. Alternatively, they can be sufficiently attractive – such as a neat cage of pussy willow twigs to support hyacinths, or a little fence of bamboo canes to support narcissi – to justify being on show. Plants such as the big regale lilies, with heavy flowering heads, will have to be supported or otherwise they will droop or snap off. Equally, very spreading plants with soft stems, such as begonias and some pelargoniums, may need a gentle, unobtrusive helping hand to create a more attractive form for the plant. Wall shrubs and climbers, like honeysuckle and some roses, will need tying on to a support, such as trellis or wires stretched across a wall or fence and fixed with vine eyes.

Young shrubs with undeveloped stems are often supported with a cane stake, to which the plant is tied. Use soft plastic ties, and ensure that they are not too tight.

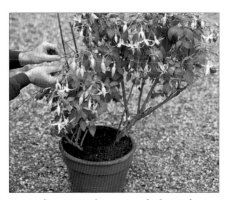

A simple system of canes, pushed into the compost or ground and fastened with wire or string can keep unruly plants in position.

A neat hoop made of linked metal stakes is useful for preventing soft-stemmed perennials from flopping over and getting damaged.

PRUNING

Most people become deeply anxious at the prospect of pruning their plants, confused by a plethora of apparently conflicting advice and unclear instructions. There are two chief principles for pruning: one is to prune a woody stemmed plant to improve its overall shape; the other is to prune it to increase the number of flowering shoots, and its consequent flower power.

Before you become hopelessly neurotic, most plants will survive without pruning, but they will produce fewer and smaller flowers, their branches may start to cross over and tangle, and their overall appearance will be less pleasing. Remember that the first need is to prune for health (by maintaining a good open shape) and the second for beauty (to get the most flowers). A few plants (*Buddlejas*, for example) do better when pruned very hard but for most plants you should aim to remove about a third of the new growth each year. With overgrown roses, cut out a third of old stems at base level, to allow new stems to flourish.

Lopsided stems
To maintain the framework of the plant, cut back over-vigorous shoots lightly. Do not prune too hard, as this will stimulate growth.

Congested stems
Remove up to one-third of the stems from a congested plant to encourage air flow and deter pests and diseases.

Weak stems
Cut out any weak, straggly stems as these are more vulnerable to attack by pests and diseases.

Pruning for Shape

This kind of pruning is to prevent plants becoming untidy and straggly or 'awkward' shapes. You can encourage the direction a branch takes by pruning back to a bud that is pointing in the direction you wish the shoot to grow. This will help 'open out' the centre of the plant, encouraging the air to circulate and the plant will be healthier and look better. Remove any diseased or damaged wood at the same time. Generally speaking, this kind of pruning is best done in autumn.

Pruning for Flowers

Shrubs and climbers flower at different times of the year, some of them on old wood (on flowering shoots arising from the main woody stems) and some on new wood (flowering shoots on sideshoots formed the previous year). Your pruning strategy depends on your knowing which you are dealing with!

Generally, spring-flowering shrubs and climbers flower on wood formed the previous season. Prune them once flowering stops by cutting the shoots that bore flowers back to two buds away from the main stem. If you prune these plants in spring, you will not get flowers since you will be cutting off the shoots that flower! Late summer-flowering shrubs can also be cut back after flowering in autumn, but could be pruned instead in spring (there will be time for new growth to form and flower). Some plants, such as clematis, have a range of flowering times depending on the species. To prune correctly, establish whether they are spring- or summer-flowering, then prune as above.

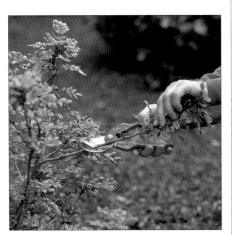

Light pruning only is all that is necessary for most evergreens, to improve the overall shape of the plant.

Pinching Out

You can encourage young plants to become more bushy if you stop the growth in the first year by removing the growing point (the leading shoot or shoots) of each plant. This encourages sideshoots to form, increasing the lateral spread of the plant. Remove the tip simply by pinching it out between finger and thumb, or with a sharp knife.

This technique is particularly valuable with plants such as box, pelargoniums, browallia, some petunias and antirrhinums.

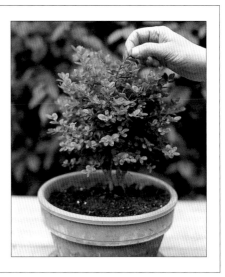

GARDEN DIY

As well as creating attractive plant groupings, you will also need to carry out certain tasks to do with the hardware of the garden: for example, fixing brackets for hanging baskets and wall pots, repairing cracked or broken containers, putting up trellis, and last, but not least, moving heavy containers.

REPAIRING POTS

If a terracotta pot shatters, you can wire it, if it has broken cleanly, under the rim of the pot. Place the pot upside down with the broken edges together. Cut a length of galvanized wire about 25cm (10in) longer than the circumference of the pot. Ask an assistant to hold the wire tight around the pot rim, while you twist the ends to form a collar. Use a screwdriver blade to tighten the collar by rotating the blade. Trim with wire cutters.

To treat more complex breaks, use epoxy putty. Mix the two materials of the epoxy putty together as instructed by the manufacturer. Work the putty into a pliable strip. Dip the pieces of terracotta pot to be joined in water. Break off a piece of putty and roll it into a long, thin sausage. Press the putty to one broken edge, and position the matching broken piece on top of it. Push together to squeeze the putty into all the crevices. Trim off excess putty and leave overnight to set. Treat additional breaks in the same way, leaving to harden in between treatments.

PAINTING POTS

Pots can be painted easily with modern acrylic paints and need little or no priming. Water-based paints are easy to use, look good and can simply be repainted after a couple of years. A little weathering, however, often adds to the attraction. To paint a pot with emulsion paint, you will need both primer and an acrylic varnish.

1 *Paint the pot using the acrylic primer. This provides a seal for the pot's surface and a surface to act as a key for the emulsion.*

2 *Then paint the pot with emulsion paint, using first one coat, and then a second when the first one dries, if needed.*

3 *Finally, apply a coat of acrylic varnish and allow to dry.*

Wet the edges of the broken pot. Using a spatula, apply epoxy putty to all broken surfaces. Press together and tape the pot to keep the pieces in place. Remove when dry.

DECORATIVE PAINT EFFECTS

Pots of all kinds can benefit from attractive decoration, and these decorations can be as simple or as elaborate as your skills and taste will allow. Simple terracotta pots look pretty with a decorated, painted rim, which is remarkably easy to create.

Alternatively, you could create a range of interesting paint effects on your pots, from crackle glaze, where the surface of the pot acquires a wonderfully 'aged' appearance, to sponging, where a runny wet painted surface is worked into with a natural sponge, or even colourwashing, where a thin layer of paint is applied that allows the textured base surface to show through.

Painting a border

1 Make a template from card or paper, using a coin as a guide for a half-circle design. Tape it to the rim.

2 Using a soft stippling brush paint the rim of the pot with a quick-drying acrylic paint.

3 When dry, you can remove the template to reveal a prettily decorated painted rim.

The finished decorated pot.

Ageing a Pot

Plain mass-produced terracotta pots look much prettier when weathered from a few seasons out-of-doors. This natural process can be speeded up using a coat of live yoghurt.

1 Apply yoghurt to the pot with a paintbrush. Set the pot out-of-doors to dry.

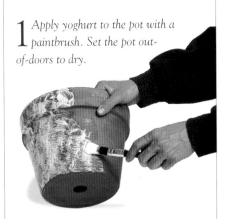

2 Once the pot looks aged, and the yoghurt has dried (after a few days), plant the pot up in the usual way.

Fixings for Hanging Baskets

Hanging baskets can be suspended from overhead swivel hooks or wall-mounted brackets. The swivel hook is usually fixed to a metal plate which is screwed to the underside of a stout piece of timber. The centre of the metal plate is threaded to take the hook, which is screwed through the plate into the wooden support. If you wish to raise and lower the hanging basket, you will need to attach a guide for a pulley to the metal plate, with a hook on the end of the pulley for the basket.

Supporting wall brackets

Wall brackets are generally made of wrought iron, and the length of the arm needs to be at least as long as half the diameter of the basket. The bracket will need to be screwed to a solid support, such as a wall or stout supporting timber. Remember that the basket is extremely heavy once filled with compost that is saturated, so ensure the support for the bracket is solid enough to hold its weight.

Fixing windowboxes

Windowboxes on upper storey windows need either a guard rail around the box or should be secured by chains to the wall, to prevent accidents. If your windows open outwards, you will need to secure the

A wire basket, filled with pansies, is suspended from a sturdy metal bracket.

windowbox to the wall using supporting brackets and similar retaining chains.

Securing safety chains

Drill holes in the masonry on the outside house wall about 30cm (12in) up from the base of the window, and about 8cm (3in) outside the window frame. Insert wall plugs and screw in strong steel hooks. Screw in heavy-duty eyes to each end of the windowbox itself at the outward facing end. Attach the windowbox to the wall using steel chain.

PLANT FINDER

Finding the right plant for the right place is the key to successful planting schemes. This section categorizes the most valuable plants into groups of most benefit to small-space gardeners. Anyone creating a planting scheme for a small space needs to look for a variety of plant forms, from small trees, climbers and shrubs

to tiny alpine plants, depending on the setting. They also need to ensure that the chosen plants will do well in the situation, since they all have different requirements.

ABOVE *Delicate flowers, like those of* Primula sieboldii, *should be planted where they can be seen in close-up to appreciate their fragile beauty.*

RIGHT *The silvery felted leaves of* Helichrysum petiolare 'Silverlight' *with its trailing habit make an excellent addition to any hanging container.*

CLIMBERS & WALL SHRUBS

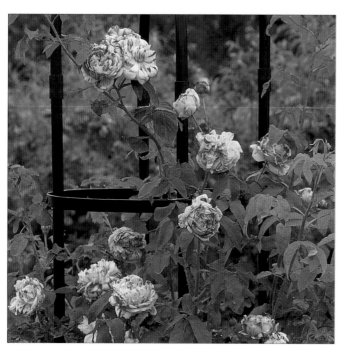

Rosa 'Variegata di Bologna'

Most small gardens boast a wall or fence, or even a balcony rail, which will provide the support necessary for an interesting variety of climbers. Their value is in the way that they will scramble up or around any support using hooks, in the case of roses for example, twining tendrils or leaf stalks, or twining stems. There is no shortage of climbers to choose from, many of them with abundant flowers in spring, summer or autumn, but the situation you have in mind should govern your choice, since some do better in shade or sun, and some in cool or hot situations.

For shady walls, the climbing hydrangea (*Hydrangea petiolaris*) or ivy (*Hedera helix*) are invaluable. For a sheltered wall, grow camellias with their glossy green leaves and marvellous oriental flowers in early spring. Sweet peas provide a short-lived but glorious display of scented flowers in full sun in summer, as do many of the climbing roses, some jasmines, and of course the ubiquitous honeysuckle, of which there are many varieties to choose from, some more glamorous in flower form, others more highly scented. A few honeysuckles will also do well in partial shade, such as *Lonicera periclymenum* and *L. × americana*.

Clematis is universally popular, with its varied flower forms from the tiny macropetala clematis to the saucer-sized hybrids, and a species can be found to flower in most months of the year. They need a shaded root run and well-drained soil to survive. More vigorous species, such as *C. montana*, will need occasional pruning to keep them under control.

Wall shrubs differ from climbers in having no actual means of supporting themselves, and they will need to be tied to a framework of wires or trellis to keep them close to the supporting wall.

Camellia
Theaceae

H 1 – 4m (3 – 12ft)

S 0.6 – 1.8m (2 – 6ft)

Beautiful, glossy leaved shrubs which prefer a lime-free soil or compost, and are ideal in containers. Although they grow well in the open, they enjoy the shelter and warmth of a wall (not east-facing, as early sun spoils frosted blooms). *C. japonica* covers a huge range of hybrids, with single, semi-double and double flowers in shades of red, pink and white.

Clematis
OLD MAN'S BEARD
Ranunculaceae

H 1.8 – 14m (6 – 46ft)

S 0.6 – 1.8m (2 – 6ft)

The huge range of clematis available means that there is a variety in flower during every month of the year. Many will ramble through other plants without causing damage, adding an extra dimension to them. Creamy-flowered, evergreen *C. cirrhosa balearica* flowers in winter, the exuberant white- or pink-flowered *C. montana* and mauve-blue *C. macropetala* in spring, and the yellow *C. tangutica* in autumn. Most of the large-flowered hybrids flower in summer. Among the most spectacular are *C.* 'Nelly Moser', with pink-striped flowers; *C.* 'Ville de Lyon', with magenta flowers and *C.* 'The President', with purple flowers.

Convolvulus
BINDWEED
Convolvulaceae

H 30 – 60cm (12 – 24in)

S 40cm (16in) or more

C. althaeoides is a hardy, vigorous twining climber, bearing pink, funnel-shaped flowers. Its spread can be restricted by planting it in a container. *C. tricolor* has tall-growing forms with royal blue flowers, with yellow and white

centres. Blooms continuously in the summer; each flower lasts only a day. Frost-tender, needing a sunny, well-drained site.

Garrya elliptica
SILK TASSEL BUSH
Garryaceae

H and S 4m (12ft)

An upright, evergreen bush with glossy, wavy-edged leaves, grown for its winter display of long, grey-green male catkins. *G.e.* 'James Roof' has clusters of silvery catkins up to 20cm (8in) long. *G.e.* 'Evie' has catkins up to 30cm (12in) long. When trained against a wall, other plants, such as clematis, can be grown through it to give colour in summer.

Hedera helix 'Glacier'
IVY
Araliaceae

H 1.8m (6ft) or more

Many of the ivies are suitable for growing against a wall, as they are tolerant of a wide range of conditions, and will support themselves as they become established. *H. h.* 'Glacier' has small, almost triangular-shaped leaves which are variegated grey-green and cream. It is useful for covering a dull wall, wooden post or fence, and it can also be grown as ground cover or as a houseplant.

Hydrangea petiolaris
CLIMBING HYDRANGEA
Hydrangeaceae

H 10m (30ft)

A deciduous, woody climber, which supports itself against a wall or fence as it grows by means of aerial roots. It has flattened white flowerheads in summer, consisting of both fertile and sterile florets. The long, heart-shaped leaves are dark green, turning golden-yellow in autumn. It prefers moist soil and shelter from cold winds, but is fully hardy and tolerant of shade.

Jasminum
JASMINE
Oleaceae
H and **S** 3m (10ft)

J. nudiflorum (winter jasmine) is a floppy, deciduous shrub producing masses of fragrant, golden-yellow flowers in winter. It needs tying to its support, but will soon cover the lower part of a wall. *J. humile* bears bright yellow, sometimes scented, flowers from late spring to early autumn. *J. officinale* (common jasmine) is a twining deciduous climber which produces clusters of highly scented white flowers in summer. All prefer full sun or partial shade and a moist soil.

Lathyrus odoratus
SWEET PEA
Leguminosae
H 0.6 – 2.5m (2 – 8ft)
S 45cm (18in)

Many cultivars and hybrids have been developed from these annual climbers with their distinctive scent. They climb, by means of tendrils, against walls and fences, or over other plants, preferring full sun and a fertile soil or compost. Flower colours include red, salmon, pink, purple, violet and white, in solid colours, shades or picotee (i.e. darker edging). Excellent as cut flowers.

Lonicera periclymenum
EARLY DUTCH
HONEYSUCKLE
Caprifoliaceae
H up to 7m (22ft)

A vigorous climber with twining, woody stems which need supporting against a wall, but will twist around trellis or the stems of other plants. This is one of the first honeysuckles to flower (mid-spring to midsummer). It produces tubular white flowers which age to yellow, with a red reverse to the petals. Likes a well-drained soil and full sun or partial shade. *L.p.* 'Serotina', or Late Dutch honeysuckle, has creamy white flowers streaked with dark red-purple.

Parthenocissus tricuspidata
BOSTON IVY
Vitaceae
H 10m (30ft)

This is a vigorous, woody climber which supports itself by means of tiny sucker pads at the tips of the tendrils. Its leaves are three-lobed and bright green, turning fiery-red to purple in autumn. *P.t.* 'Beverley Brook' has purple-green foliage, turning bright red in autumn. *P.t.* 'Veitchii' has purple-red autumn colours. Tolerates sun or shade in a well-drained soil.

Pyracantha
FIRETHORN
Rosaceae
H and **S** 3m (10ft)

Tolerant, spiny, evergreen shrub with mid- to dark-green leaves and white flowers in spring, followed by berries in autumn. Berry colour varies: those of *P.* 'Mohave' are red-orange, *P.* 'Shawnee' are orange-yellow, *P.* 'Soleil d'Or' are golden-yellow, and *P. × watereri* are red.

Prunes back well against a wall or fence, and supports other climbers grown through it.

Rosa
ROSE
Rosaceae
H 3m (10ft) **S** 2.5m (8ft)

Climbing roses have vigorous, stiff stems with glossy foliage. Some flower once in summer, others repeatedly. *R.* 'New Dawn' has repeat, double flowers of pale pink. *R.* 'Maigold' has semi-double yellow flowers in one main flush, followed by a sparse second. *R.* 'Mme Alfred Carrière' has double pale-pink to white flowers from summer to autumn. (See also page 133, SEASONAL COLOUR: SUMMER).

Solanum crispum
CHILEAN POTATO TREE
Solanaceae
H 3m (10ft) **S** 1.8m (6ft)

A scrambling evergreen or semi-evergreen climber which needs supporting against a wall or fence. It has dark green leaves and fragrant purple flowers in clusters at the end of the stems, followed by pale yellow fruit. *S.c.* 'Glasnevin' has dark purple-blue flowers from summer to autumn. Grow in full sun, and protect the plant in winter, as it is not frost-hardy.

Thunbergia alata
BLACK-EYED SUSAN
Acanthaceae
H 1.5 – 3m (5 – 10ft)

Generally grown as a trailing annual, this plant is actually a climbing perennial. It produces a profusion of orange, yellow or cream flowers with purple-brown centres throughout summer and autumn. As it is not hardy, protection will be required over winter, so growing it in a container will allow it to be moved indoors or into a conservatory until the following year.

Lathyrus odoratus 'Spencer Hybrids mixed'

Clematis macropetala 'Maidwell Hall'

Jasminum humile 'Revolution'

Lonicera periclymenum 'Serotina'

Solanum crispum 'Glasnevin'

FEATURE PLANTS

Hydrangea macrophylla

Plants that have particularly handsome attributes of form can be described as having architectural merit. Even in small gardens, these striking plants have their uses. Just because a garden is limited in size does not mean that you have to think small in terms of plants. A good architectural plant, sited in a corner, alcove or at a focal point in the garden changes the dimensions of the garden and gives it a change of scale and pace.

By virtue of their size and form, these plants can be sited in solitary positions, often slightly raised above the rest of the planting, to make a strong statement.

Among the best architectural foliage plants are those with either large leaves or interesting leaf forms. The sword- and fan-shaped leaves of yuccas, phormiums and cordylines, which are often distinctively marked, look particularly good in raised containers. Equally strong in form are big artichokes and thistles, some well over 2m (6ft 6in) tall and with steely-blue foliage. Slightly softer in form are the tall shapes and softer leaves of the plume poppy (*Macleaya cordata*).

Of the architectural flowering plants, the big trumpet-shaped flowers of the tender Angel's trumpet (*Brugmansia* sp.) and the wonderfully scented, similarly trumpet-shaped flowers of *Lilium regale* make wonderful additions, in matched pairs, to a summer doorway or terrace.

On a smaller scale, the clump-forming, starry blue flowers of *Agapanthus* make excellent specimen container plants, as do the huge cloud-like heads of purple flowers and strap-like leaves of the big allium, *A. christophii*.

Agapanthus
AFRICAN BLUE LILY
Alliaceae
H 40 – 120cm (16 – 48in)
S 30 – 60cm (12 – 24in)

These attractive, dramatic perennials form clumps of arching, strap-like leaves of a rich green. The rounded flowerheads are produced on tall stems, with the individual bell- or trumpet-shaped flowers being held aloft or drooping down, according to variety. A. 'Liliput' and A. 'Midnight Blue' with deep blue flowers are smaller varieties suitable for growing in containers. A. 'Headbourne Hybrids' has funnel-shaped flowers in shades of purple, blue and white.

Allium christophii
ONION
Alliaceae
H 30 – 60cm (12 – 24in)
S 15 – 18cm (6 – 7in)

The strap-like, grey-green leaves of this perennial grow up from the bulbous base and are fringed with short, stiff hairs. These begin to die back almost before the globe-shaped flowerheads appear in early summer. Each head consists of up to 50 star-shaped, metallic, pinkish-purple flowers, which can be cut and dried for use in indoor flower arrangements. At 10 – 25cm

(4 – 10in) high, A. *karataviense* is smaller and one of the few onions whose leaves are as attractive as its flowers. Its size makes it ideal for smaller containers. Pairs of broad leaves grow from the basal bulb, each leaf forming a wide arc. The leaves are greenish-purple in colour, with red edges. Umbels of pale pink, star-shaped flowers are borne in summer on red-tinted stems.

Brugmansia × candida
ANGEL'S TRUMPETS
Solanaceae
H 1.2 – 1.8m (4 – 6ft)
S 1.8 – 2.4m (6 – 8ft)

Brugmansia is not fully hardy outdoors, but will thrive in a protected position away from frost. It is a large plant, ideal for a conservatory where its spectacular, fragrant, trumpet-shaped flowers can be fully appreciated. These are produced throughout summer and autumn and come in shades of apricot (B. × c. 'Grand Marnier') and white (B. × c. 'Double White').

Canna × generalis
INDIAN SHOT PLANT
Cannaceae
H 1.5 – 2.2m (5 – 7ft)
S 50cm (20in)

Tall, exotic-looking herbaceous perennials with orchid-like flowers, growing from slowly-spreading rhizomes. They prefer moist soil in full sun, and

Agapanthus hybrid

Canna 'General Eisenhower'

provide colour and height where space is limited. Numerous hybrids have foliage colours varying from green to bronze, and flower colours including yellow, orange, red, coral and salmon. They will need protection over winter.

Cordyline australis
CABBAGE PALM
Agavaceae
H 1m (3ft) in pots s 1m (3ft)

A slow-growing, half-hardy tree, it can grow to 7m (25ft) when planted in soil. The strap-shaped leaves are borne at the tip of a narrow stem, and form an arching cluster. Older trees bear long plume-like panicles of creamy flowers in summer.

Fritillaria imperialis
CROWN IMPERIAL
Liliaceae
H 60 – 90cm (2 – 3ft)
s 45cm (18in)

This handsome spring-flowering bulb has lance-shaped green leaves, which curl over at the tip from the centre of which a spire of tulip-shaped drooping flowers in yellow to orange-red is borne in mid-spring. Will do well in sun or partial shade.

Helianthus annuus
SUNFLOWER
Compositae
H 0.6 – 5m (2 – 15ft)
s up to 1.2m (4ft)

Sunflowers come in shades of gold, yellow and orange, and in a wide range of heights. *H.a.* 'Sunspot' has 25cm (10in) yellow flowers on 60cm (2ft) stems, *H.a.* 'Teddy Bear' has 13cm (5in) double, deep-yellow flowers on 90cm (3ft) stems. Many are unbranching, although some, such as *H.a.* 'Music Box' branch freely, and have numerous flowers.

Hydrangea macrophylla
COMMON HYDRANGEA
Hydrangeaceae
H 1 – 2m (3 – 6ft) s 1.5m (5ft)
Rounded, deciduous shrubs preferring moist soil. They are

divided into two groups according to the flowers: lace-caps (flattened clusters of tiny fertile flowers surrounded by a ring of larger sterile ones), such as 'Blue Wave', and mop-heads (or Hortensias, with a spherical head of larger sterile flowers), such as dark blue 'Europa'. Flower colours of blue, white and pink are influenced by soil acidity, blue requiring the more acid soil.

Lilium regale
REGAL LILY
Liliaceae
H 0.6 – 1.8m (2 – 6ft)
s 15 – 20cm (6 – 8in)

From a dull-looking bulb, lilies produce the most spectacular flowers in summer. Those of the regal lily are large and trumpet-shaped, highly fragrant, and produced in clusters of up to 25 at the top of the stem. Pinkish in bud, they open white with a pinkish-purple reverse and yellow centre with golden anthers. They prefer full sun and a well-drained soil.

Macleaya microcarpa
PLUME POPPY
Papaveraceae
H 2.2m (7ft) s 1m (3ft)

This rhizomatous perennial has graceful, heart-shaped, grey-green foliage and delicate grass-like flowers on tall stems. The tube-like, petal-less flowers are carried in plumes. *M.m.* 'Kelway's Coral Plume' has

coral-pink flowers in early summer. An invasive plant, it is best kept in a container, and will need regular repotting.

Melianthus major
HONEY BUSH
Melianthaceae
H 1.8 – 3m (6 – 10ft)
s 1 – 3m (3 – 10ft)

A strong specimen shrub with hollow stems set near ground level. It has spreading, grey- to blue-green pinnate leaves, each deeply toothed. The small, tube-shaped, deep brownish-red flowers are borne in early summer on tall spikes. Melianthus is not frost-hardy.

Phormium tenax
NEW ZEALAND FLAX
Phormiaceae
H 3m (10ft) s 1.2m (4ft)

A half-hardy evergreen perennial, *P. tenax* is grown for

Lilium regale

Macleaya microcarpa

its tall sword-shape leaves. *P.t.* 'Purpureum' has bronze-purple foliage and *P.t.* 'Variegatum' has yellow/green striped leaves. The flowers, a dull red, are carried in long panicles between summer and autumn.

Yucca filamentosa
ADAM'S NEEDLE
Agavaceae
H 1.8m (6ft) s 1.5m (5ft)

A dramatic, stemless, evergreen shrub, forming a rosette of long, rigid, lance-shaped leaves of a dark green edged with curly white threads. A tall spike of white, bell-shaped flowers may be produced in summer. Grow in full sun. *Y.f.* 'Bright Edge' has yellow-edges to the leaves; *Y.f.* 'Variegata' has white-edged, blue-green leaves. *Y. gloriosa* has darker leaves and is larger. It flowers later in the year and only when about five years old.

Melianthus major

Helianthus annuus

Yucca gloriosa

FOLIAGE PLANTS

Often forgotten in the hectic rush to include flower colour, foliage plays an essential part in giving a garden, no matter how small, a backcloth against which the flowers can be seen to full advantage, and, where the leaves are particularly striking (see Feature Plants, pages 122-3) makes a valuable contribution to the overall design features of the garden.

Foliage comes in many forms, textures and colours. The selection here simply aims to give a taste of the myriad different types available, from the tiny evergreen leaves of box (*Buxus sempervirens*) or the neat oval leaves of bay (*Laurus nobilis*) which lend themselves to being clipped into neat topiary forms, to the conical form of the dwarf cypress and the marvellous crenellate fronds of ferns such as *Asplenium* and *Polypodium*.

Many foliage plants will thrive in shady areas of the garden where you would have considerable difficulty persuading flowering plants to flourish. Among these are plants like ivy (*Hedera* sp.) which has a wonderfully diverse range of leaf forms from the long, narrow leaves of *Hedera sagittifolia* to the big, cream-splashed leaves of the more tender *Hedera helix* 'Glacier'.

Silvery felted leaves make a contribution to the dry garden, their furry coating enabling them to stand up well to drought. Many of these silver- or furry-leaved plants are herbs (wormwood and sage spring to mind) but the silvery-leaved senecios are excellent for containers and make a wonderful foil for purple- or blue-flowered plants.

Hedera helix 'Pedata'

Alchemilla mollis
LADY'S MANTLE
Rosaceae
H 60cm (24in)
S 75cm (30in)

A clump-forming perennial with rounded, soft green leaves which are covered with fine, silky hairs. It is drought-tolerant and makes an excellent ground-cover plant. Loose clusters of tiny, greenish-yellow flowers are produced throughout the summer. Grow the plant in moist soil in full sun or partial shade, and remove the dead flowerheads regularly to prevent seeding.

Asplenium scolopendrium
HART'S TONGUE FERN
Aspleniaceae
H 45 – 70cm (17 – 28in)
S 60cm (24in)

A distinctive evergreen fern, this plant has bright green, wavy, strap-like fronds, with slightly frilled edges, a pointed tip and a heart-shaped base. It is hardy, and enjoys a moist soil in partial shade. In a container, extra grit may be added to the compost to ensure adequate drainage. *A.s. Crispum* Group has very frilled edges to the leaves.

Buxus sempervirens
BOX, BOXWOOD
Buxaceae
H 3m (10ft)
S 1.2 – 1.8m (4 – 6ft)

A hardy, slow-growing, bushy evergreen plant with small, oval-shaped, glossy, dark green leaves. Often used for hedging, it is useful as a foil to more brightly coloured plants, and attractive in its variegated forms of *B.s.* 'Elegantissima' (white-edged leaves) and *B.s.* 'Marginata' (yellow-edged leaves). Used singly in a container, its main attraction is that it can easily be clipped to form topiary.

Chamaecyparis
DWARF CYPRESS
Cupressaceae
H 1 – 1.5m (3 – 5ft)
S up to 1m (3ft)

Cypresses are ideal at providing structure in a plant display because they remain evergreen throughout the year. They come in all shapes, sizes and colours, but where space is limited, only truly dwarf ones should be chosen. *C. lawsoniana* 'Minima' has blue-green foliage and a round habit. *C. obtusa* 'Nana Aurea' has golden foliage and a flattened, upright habit. *C. obtusa* 'Pygmaea' has green foliage in flattened sprays.

Euphorbia characias subsp. wulfenii
SPURGE
Euphorbiaceae
H and S 1.2m (4ft)

An upright, evergreen shrub with grey-green leaves on purple-tinted stems, preferring moist soil and partial shade. Each stem grows one year and flowers the next – and should then be cut off unless the seed is wanted. The unusual flowers are borne in rounded clusters at the tips of the stems, and are yellow-green in colour. *E.c. subsp. characias* has handsome green flowers with deep purple centres.

Hedera helix
COMMON IVY
Araliaceae
H 10cm (4in)
S 1m (3ft) or more

The small-leaved ivies look exceptionally good in tall containers or hanging baskets, where they can trail gracefully. Choose varieties with leaves to complement the planting. All are tolerant of a wide range of conditions. *H.h.* 'Goldchild' has a broad yellow margin around each grey-green leaf, *H.h.* 'Eva' has small, grey-green leaves with creamy-white edges, and *H.h.* 'Ivalace' has wavy, glossy, dark

...lenium scolopendrium

Buxus sempervirens

Euphorbia characias subsp. *wulfenii*

...en leaves. (See also page 120,
...MBERS AND WALL SHRUBS).

**...euchera micrantha
...alace Purple'**
...RAL FLOWER
...ifragaceae
...0 – 45cm (12 – 18in)
...0cm (12in)
...erbaceous perennial, this is
...l worth growing for its
...ndsome maple-like deep
...ple leaves and deep maroon
...vers. Will cope with sun or
...tial shade but prefers light,
...ll-drained soil. Use as either a
...ntainer-grown feature plant or
...edging.

**...osta sieboldiana
...legans'**
...ANTAIN LILY
...nkiaceae
...m (3ft) **s** 1.2m (4ft)
...ong-lived perennial which
...ms a clump of thick, ribbed,
...rt-shaped, blue-green leaves.
...ows best where it has moist
...l and partial shade, especially
...m midday sun. Bell-shaped,
...uve flowers are produced on
...l stems in summer. The
...ghtly smaller variety
...s. 'Frances Williams' has
...y-white flowers and thick,
...rt-shaped leaves, drawn
...nd to form a cup. They are
...bed and puckered, blue-green
...the centre with a lighter
...llow-green edge. Hostas

associate well with water, but
will grow in containers as long
as they are well watered and fed.

Laurus nobilis
BAY
Lauraceae
H 5m (16ft) **s** 3m (10ft)
As well as lending its
distinctive, warm aroma to
cooking, bay makes an
attractive specimen plant and
can be shaped as it grows into a
pyramid, ball or standard. It
needs a sunny or partially-
shaded position away from cold
winds and, in colder areas, will
need some winter protection.
The leaves are aromatic, glossy
and dark green, the flowers are
small and greenish-yellow.

Polypodium vulgare
COMMON POLYPODY
Polypodiaceae
H 30cm (12in) **s** indefinite
A typical evergreen fern, with
arching, dark green fronds 40cm
(16in) long, divided into oblong
pinnae. It enjoys full sun or light
shade amongst other plants, or
standing alone as a specimen.
Unlike some ferns, it is fully
hardy, although protection may
be needed around the base of
the container in very low temperatures to protect the roots.
The variety 'Cornubiense' is
very vigorous, and makes good
ground cover.

**Senecio cineraria
'Silver Dust'**
Compositae
H and **s** 30cm (12in)
An evergreen subshrub, usually
grown as an annual and
discarded at the end of the
summer. The lacy, deeply-
divided leaves are covered in a
grey-white felt, giving the
whole plant a silvery-white
appearance. Small yellow
flowers appear in the second
summer after planting.
S.c. 'Alice' has deeply cut
silvery-white leaves; *S.c.* 'White
Diamond' has oak-like
greyish-white leaves. The
plant prefers a sunny position
and tolerates slightly dry
conditions, and so is good for
hanging baskets.

Vinca minor
LESSER PERIWINKLE
Apocynaceae
H 10 – 20cm (4 – 8in)
s indefinite
A hardy, spreading evergreen,
with long, trailing stems which
root as they grow, bearing small,
oval-shaped, dark green leaves
and trumpet-shaped flowers of
blue, purple, reddish-purple or
white. *V.m.* 'Azurea Flore
Pleno' has double, light blue
flowers. *V.m.* 'Gertrude Jekyll' is
compact with white flowers.
V.m. 'La Grave' has large,
lavender-coloured flowers.

Heuchera micrantha 'Palace
Purple'

Hosta fortunei 'Francee'

125

TRAILING PLANTS

Among the most useful plants in a small garden are those with a trailing habit, both for foliage or flowers. They make excellent candidates for all forms of container, but particularly for hanging baskets where they can be persuaded to create wonderfully relaxed plantings, in a range of delicious colours and colour mixtures.

Of the trailing flowering plants, some forms of begonia, pelargonium, petunia, convolvulus, lobelia, diascia and felicia are highly popular flowering plants in a marvellous mixture of colours and flower shapes, from the tiny starry flowers of lobelia to the soft-petalled blooms of convolvulus, the waxy almost oriental quality of begonias through to the rather blowzy big flowers of slightly scented petunias.

Of the trailing leaves, those of helichrysum, ivy and vinca, as well as those of nasturtiums (*Tropaeolum majus*) can be used to soften the edges of containers, or trail elegantly from the top of walls, for example. Any mixed planting is most successful if the balance between foliage form and flower power is maintained.

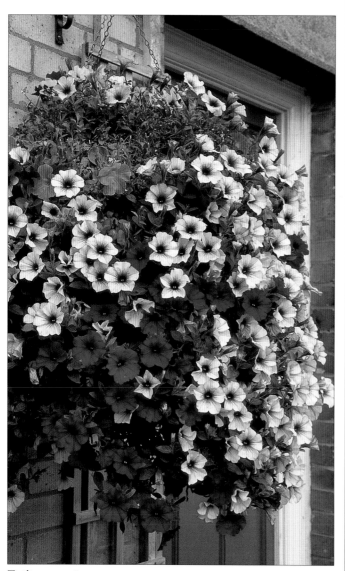

Trailing petunias

Begonia
Begoniaceae

H 15 – 60cm (6 – 24in)
S 15 – 45cm (6 – 18in)

The trailing Pendulas (single to double) are excellent for containers or hanging baskets. Other summer-flowering begonias hardy enough to survive outdoors are the Tuberous Begonias, grouped as large-flowered Tuberhybridas (usually double-flowered), the smaller-flowered *Multifloras* (single to double), and *Semperflorens*, which are smaller, with a profusion of (usually) single flowers. Foliage is green to bronze, and flower shades include red, pink, orange, yellow and white, depending on variety.

Brachyscome
SWAN RIVER DAISY
Compositae

H 30 – 45cm (12 – 18in)
S 35 – 45cm (14 – 18in)

Finely leaved plants which produce masses of small, daisy-like flowers in summer. They are fairly drought-tolerant, making them useful in hanging baskets. *B. iberidifolia* is bushy or spreading, with soft, grey foliage and fragrant blue, pink or white, yellow-centred flowers. *B.i.* Splendour Series has white, pink or purple, black-centred flowers. *B. multifida* produces fewer flowers in blue, pink, mauve, purple and white.

Convolvulus sabatius
BINDWEED
Convolvulaceae

H 15cm (6in) S 50cm (20in)

A tolerant, slender, trailing perennial, sometimes grown as an annual, with small, bright green leaves and funnel-shaped flowers, ranging from very pale to rich, deep purple-blue. These are produced in clusters of up to three throughout the summer and early autumn. Overwinter in a cold greenhouse for cuttings or division in spring. Smaller,

Begonia semperflorens

bushy varieties of convolvulus thrive in containers. *C. cneorum* has silky, silver-coloured leaves and flowers which are pink in bud, opening white. It prefers a sunny, well-drained site and needs frost protection. (See also page 120, CLIMBERS AND WALL SHRUBS).

Diascia
Scrophulariaceae

H up to 30cm (12in)
S 20 – 30cm (8 – 12in)

Trailing or upright, pretty evergreen, or semi-evergreen, mat-forming perennials. They prefer a sunny site and have a long flowering season, bearing a profusion of tubular flowers with backward-facing spurs. *D.* 'Pink Queen' trails, bearing masses of pink, long-spurred flowers; *D. rigescens* is more upright, with deep pink flowers, and *D.* 'Ruby Field' is more compact, with rich, salmon-pink flowers.

Felicia
BLUE DAISY
Compositae

H 30 – 60cm (12 – 24in)

Grown mainly for their outstanding display of long-stalked, daisy-like flowers with yellow centres, these are excellent plants for the hanging basket as they enjoy slightly dry conditions and a sunny position. *F. amelloides* is a small, bushy subshrub with deep green leaves

Brachyscome multifida

Convolvulus sabatius

Felicia amelloides

and light to dark blue flowers throughout summer and early autumn. *F.a.* 'Read's White' has white flowers, *F.a.* 'Santa Anita' produces large, vivid blue flowers, and *F. amoena* 'Variegata' has cream-marked leaves and blue flowers.

Fuchsia
Onagraceae
H 15 – 30cm (6 – 12in)
S 46 – 60cm (18 – 24in)

Choose only very small trailing types (or bush fuchsias) for use in hanging baskets. Tolerant of full sun or partial shade, they prefer shelter from cold winds. *F.* 'Marinka' is a trailing variety with dark green leaves and shaded red flowers. *F.* 'Lady Thumb' is a small upright bush with small, semi-double flowers of rose-pink and white.

Helichrysum petiolare
Compositae
H up to 15cm (6in)
S 60cm (24in)

A frost-tender, trailing, evergreen shrub with branching stems and woolly, heart-shaped leaves. Grown mainly for its pretty foliage, it does produce small whitish flowers in late summer. Prefers a sheltered position in full sun, and will tolerate slightly dry conditions. *H.p.* 'Aurea' (syn. *H.p.* 'Limelight') has bright, lime-green foliage, *H.p.* 'Variegatum'

has grey-green leaves, variegated with cream. *H. p.* 'Silverlight' has felted grey leaves.

Impatiens
See page 132, SEASONAL COLOUR.

Lantana camara
Verbenaceae
H and **S** 1m (3ft)

The leaves of this sun-loving, evergreen shrub are rough and dull green, but the clusters of flowers are bright and colourful, changing from pale yellow to salmon, red and purple as they age. *L.c.* 'Cream Carpet' is smaller, with creamy white flowers, *L.c.* 'Feston Rose' has pink and yellow flowerheads, and *L.c.* 'Goldmine' has golden yellow flowerheads.

Lobelia erinus
Campanulaceae
H 10 – 23cm (4 – 9in)
S 10 – 15cm (4 – 6in)

Bushy, low-growing or trailing plants grown as annuals with green or bronze foliage, bearing masses of small white, pink, red, violet, purple or blue flowers throughout summer and autumn. *L.e. Cascade* and Regatta Series are both trailing, *L.e.* 'Crystal Palace' has dark blue flowers, *L.e.* 'Rosamund' has cherry-red flowers with a white centre and *L.e.* 'Minstrel' has bright blue flowers with a white centre.

Helichrysum petiolare 'Silverlight'

Lantana camara 'Goldmine'

Lobelia 'Minstrel'

Variegated pelargonium

Petunia 'Vogue'

Tropaeolum 'Apricot Twist'

Verbena 'Silver Anne'

Mimulus
MONKEY FLOWER
Scrophulariaceae
H 15 – 30cm (6 – 12in)
S 30cm (12in)
Bushy, spreading plants, perennial or annual, which enjoy a warm, sunny position. They produce trumpet-shaped flowers throughout the summer. Tender M. × *hybridus* cultivars, including 'Calypso', bear single-coloured, spotted and bicoloured flowers in red, pink, orange and yellow, and the Magic Series includes unusual pastel shades as well as bright oranges, yellows and reds. M. 'Wisley Red' has velvety, dark red flowers.

Pelargonium
GERANIUM
Geraniaceae
H and **S** up to 45cm (18in)
The trailing ivy-leaved pelargoniums are especially useful in pots or hanging baskets. Their foliage may be plain, variegated with cream or

yellow or marked with red. Flower colours include red, salmon, pink, violet or white. They are tolerant of a range of conditions, although they prefer full sun or partial shade. P. 'L'Elégante' has cream-variegated silvery green leaves which turn purplish if the plant is dry. P. 'Abel Carriere' has semi-double light purple flowers. P. 'Jacky' has semi-double lavender pink flowers and small leaves. (See also page 133, SEASONAL COLOUR: SUMMER).

Petunia
Solanaceae
H up to 30cm (12in)
S up to 1m (3ft)
Tolerant, reliable plants, which produce flowers constantly throughout the summer, preferably in full sun and sheltered from cold winds. Cascade Series has long, trailing stems. *Grandiflora* petunias have fewer, larger flowers than *Multiflora* types, which are more

bushy, with plenty of smaller flowers. P. 'Celebrity Chiffon Morn' has soft, salmon-pink flowers, P. 'Prism Sunshine' has large, light yellow flowers, and P. 'Vogue' has large light mauve flowers.

Scaevola aemula
FAIRY FAN FLOWER
Goodeniaceae
H 15cm (6in) **S** 1.5m (5ft)
An evergreen perennial, usually grown as an annual, with slightly hairy trailing or upright stems. The fan-shaped flowers are borne during the summer, and are blue to purple-blue. S.a. 'Blue Wonder' has vigorous trailing stems and a profusion of lilac-blue flowers all summer. S. 'Mauve Clusters' also has a trailing habit, and lilac-mauve flowers during summer and early autumn.

Thunbergia alata
See page 121, CLIMBERS AND WALL SHRUBS

Tropaeolum majus
NASTURTIUM
Tropaeolaceae
H 1 – 3m (3 – 10ft)
S 1.5 – 3m (5 – 10ft)
A vigorous trailing or climbing plant with rounded, light green leaves and spurred flowers throughout summer and autumn in shades of yellow, orange and red. The flowers are edible and look wonderful in a salad. T. Alaska Series are dwarf, bushy annuals with cream-flecked leaves and yellow, orange, cream and brown-red. T. 'Peach Melba' has semi-double yellow flowers with orange-red centres. T. 'Apricot Twist' is double-flowered.

Verbena
Verbenaceae
H 20cm (8in) **S** 1m (3ft)
Spreading perennials with toothed, mid-green leaves and masses of red, salmon, pink, white, purple or yellow flowers in the summer, borne in flattened clusters. They prefer a sunny position and need winter protection. V. 'Lawrence Johnson' has rich red flowers in large clusters. V. 'Sissinghurst' has dark green leaves and magenta-pink flowers. V. 'Loveliness' has flowers of a pale lavender colour. V. 'Silver Anne' produces bright pink, sweetly scented flowers which fade to silver-white as they age.

Vinca minor
See page 125, FOLIAGE PLANTS

SPREADING PLANTS

Small spreading plants are ideal for filling in small corners, cracks and crevices but they can equally well be used in small containers as special interest plants in a miniature setting. Little pots of sedums with their succulent leaves make a wonderful textural contribution, while the small brilliantly coloured flowers of aubrieta, in mauves, pinks or blues, cascade from the top of any wall. The little silvery deadnettle (*Lamium maculatum* 'Beacon Silver') makes an excellent foil for mauve flowers, while *Tiarella cordifollia* will spread and do well in shade. Erigeron makes an excellent crevice-filler. It will grow in between the cracks in paving stones, softening their appearance, and will survive being crushed underfoot.

Erigeron glaucus

Ajuga reptans
BUGLE
Labiatae
H 2 – 30cm (4 – 12in)
S 30cm (12in)
This little creeping perennial makes excellent ground cover or edging. It has deep green oblong leaves and blue flowers in summer. A purple-leaved variety, 'Burgundy Glow', is particularly attractive. It does best in partial shade.

Alyssum
Cruciferae
H 10 – 15cm (4 – 6in)
S 60cm (24in)
Mat- or clump-forming evergreen perennials, with grey-green leaves and tiny, yellow or white flowers in early summer. Prefers full sun and well-drained soil. *A. montanum* 'Berggold' has golden flowers, *A. spinosum* has white flowers and silvery leaves and *A.s. var. roseum* has pale to deep rose-pink flowers.

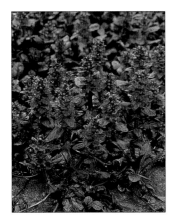

Ajuga reptans

Arabis caucasica
ROCK CRESS
Cruciferae
H 15cm (6in) **S** 50cm (20in)
A vigorous, evergreen, mat-forming perennial which is fully hardy and will grow well in any well-drained soil in full sun. Loose clusters of fragrant, white flowers are produced in late spring above the grey-green foliage. *A.c.* 'Flore Pleno' has double flowers, *A.c.* 'Variegata' has green leaves with yellow edges. *A. × arendsii* 'Rosabella' has deep rose-pink flowers.

Aubrieta × cultorum
AUBRETIA
Cruciferae
H 5cm (2in) **S** 60cm (24in)
Evergreen, spreading perennials with mid-green leaves and four-petalled flowers in spring. Grow in full sun in a well-drained soil on banks or walls. Forms include 'Argenteovariegata' (white leaf edging, single mauve flowers), 'Aureovariegata' (gold-edged leaves, single mauve flowers), 'Bressingham Pink' (double pink flowers), 'Joy' (double mauve flowers) and 'J.S. Baker' (single purple flowers with white eyes).

Erigeron
FLEABANE
Compositae
H 5 – 60cm (2 – 24in)
S 30 – 45cm (12 – 18in)
Ranging from small alpines to taller clump-forming species, they prefer full sun and a moist soil. *E. karvinskianus* is a vigorous, carpeting perennial with yellow-centred flowers which open white and fade to pink. *E. chrysopsidis* 'Grand Ridge' is mat-forming and dense, with deep-yellow flowers produced during the summer. *E. glaucus* has pale mauve flowers with yellow centres from late spring to summer.

Lamium maculatum
DEAD NETTLE
Labiatae
H 20cm (8in) **S** 1m (3ft)
A low-growing, spreading perennial with medium-large, heart-shaped, toothed leaves, often marked with splashes of other colours. The flowers appear in late spring, but the foliage is attractive in a hanging basket. Tolerates partial shade. *L.m. album* has silvery markings on the leaves, *L.m.* 'Aureum' has yellow leaves with whitish centres, and *L.m.* 'Beacon Silver' has silver leaves with a narrow green edge.

Sedum
STONECROP
Crassulaceae
H 25cm (10in) **S** 45cm (18in)
Hardy, mat-forming perennials bearing star-shaped yellow or white flowers in summer and autumn. They prefer full sun and neutral to alkaline soil. *S. acre* is very low-growing, with yellow flowers. *S.* 'Ruby Glow' has red stems and green-purple leaves and red flowers during summer and autumn. *S. spectabile* (ice plant) is taller, producing flattened heads of pink flowers above succulent-looking leaves.

Sempervivum
HOUSELEEK
Crassulaceae
H 8 – 10cm (3 – 4in)
S 30cm (12in)
Hardy, mat-forming perennials with rosettes of succulent leaves, sometimes covered with fine white webbing. Flat heads of star-shaped flowers, of yellow, white, red or purple are produced in summer. Grow in full sun in a well-drained soil. *S. arachnoideum* has reddish-coloured leaves and pink flowers. *S. giuseppii* has bright green leaves with red tips and red flowers.

Tiarella cordifolia
FOAM FLOWER
Saxifragaceae
H 10 – 30cm (4 – 12in)
S 30 – 45cm (12 – 18in)
A vigorous, hardy, herbaceous perennial which is excellent as ground cover and also in hanging baskets. It spreads by means of stolons, and prefers cool, moist (but not water-logged) conditions and partial or full shade. The low-growing, lobed, heart-shaped leaves are pale green, turning reddish in autumn. Loose spikes of tiny, creamy white flowers are produced throughout summer.

SEASONAL COLOUR

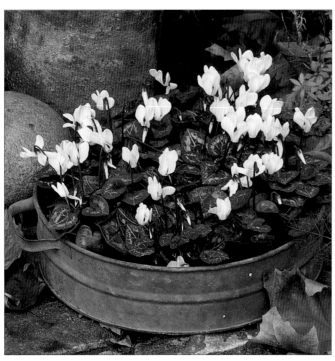

Winter-flowering cyclamen

The main aim in any small space is to ensure that there is something of interest, in terms of flowers or foliage, at different times of the year. A garden that has only one flowering season is very dismal for the remainder of the year, and in a small space it is particularly important to ensure that you have a good spread of continuous flower colour, although inevitably winter has less to offer than summer.

Spring, nonetheless, with its selection of spring bulbs, in clear colours and with fresh green leaves, offers a wide range of choice from the first snowdrops and crocuses through to the tiny, sweetly scented little narcissus, small brilliantly coloured tulips and little starry scillas in the form of bulbs, with primulas and violas playing an equally important role in mid-spring.

Summer offers a marvellous range of flowering plants, some annuals, some perennials and some flowering shrubs. Little scented pinks, exotic-looking gazanias, and brilliant coloured daisies and marigolds all help to create a highly colourful summer pageant, backed up with the gentler shades of more cloud-like flowers of shrubs like catmint. Small patio roses have been increasingly bred, providing a wide choice of sufficiently small roses for tiny balconies or even windowsills.

Autumn and winter have a smaller range of plants to offer, but their very scarcity makes them a great joy to behold. The dying embers of summer are echoed in the hot colours of chrysanthemums and dahlias in autumn. Little cyclamen with their delicately marked deep green leaves, the tiny winter iris, *I. unguicularis*, and little winter-flowering pansies and scented shrubs like mahonia and witch hazel help to perfume the garden in winter.

SPRING

Convallaria majalis
LILY OF THE VALLEY
Convallariaceae
H 23cm (9in) **S** 5cm (2in)
Hardy perennials with large, oval, pointed leaves, preferring partial shade, and spreading by means of rhizomatous, underground stems. Produces upright stalks bearing hanging, waxy, bell-like flowers in spring. They are wonderfully fragrant. *C.m.* 'Albostriata' has cream-striped leaves, *C.m.* 'Flore Pleno' has double flowers, and *C.m. var. rosea* produces flowers which are a pale mauve-pink.

Crocus
Iridaceae
H up to 10cm (4in)
S 2.5 – 5cm (1 – 2in)
Small, spring- or autumn-flowering plants which grow from individual corms. Long, slender leaves are sometimes white-striped along the upper surface. Flowers are goblet-shaped, produced four or more per corm, in shades of white, yellow, blue and purple, sometimes in combination on the same plant. *C. chrysanthus*, *C. corsicus*, *C. gargaricus*, *C. minimus* and their hybrids all flower in spring. *C. × luteus* 'Dutch Yellow' is a vigorous spring-flowering crocus which requires full sun.

Erysimum (syn. Cheiranthus)
WALLFLOWER
Cruciferae
H 25 – 80cm (10 – 32in)
S 30 – 40cm (12 – 16in)
Colourful, reliable and hardy, wallflowers produce a brilliant display in spring. Flower colours include yellow, orange, red and mauve. Cultivars of *E. cheiri*, such as Bedder Series, are more compact. *E.* 'Bowles Mauve' is a perennial with mauve flowers. *E. × kewense* 'Harpur Crewe' has double yellow flowers.

Galanthus nivalis
SNOWDROP
Amaryllidaceae
H up to 23cm (9in)
S 4 – 8cm (1.5 – 3in)
Bulbous perennials, producing long, strap-like leaves and drooping flowers in spring before dying down and becoming dormant. They need a constantly moist soil, preferably in partial shade. Varieties are single, double such as G.n. 'Flore Pleno', or unusually marked, such as G.n. 'Lady Elphinstone', which has yellow markings on the inner sepals on established plants.

Helleborus
HELLEBORE
Ranunculaceae
H and **S** to 60cm (2ft) or more
Rhizomatous perennials, either producing deciduous leaves from the base, or biennial stems. Soil preference varies, but all prefer partial shade. *H. argutifolius* has sharply toothed leaves and pale green flowers, *H. foetidus* has dark green leaves and purple-edged pale green flowers, *H. niger* (Christmas rose) has large, open, white flowers, sometimes tinted pink or green. *H. orientalis* (Lenten rose) has greenish-white or purple flowers.

Convallaria majalis

Iris
Iridaceae

H up to 30cm (12in)
S 10cm (4in)

Bulbous iris tend to flower before early rhizomatous ones; both types need a well-drained soil and full sun. Producing one flower per bulb, *I. reticulata* has pale to deep violet-blue or red-purple petals with a yellow marking on each fall (lower petal), and *I. danfordiae* has yellow with green markings. Hybrids include *I.* 'Apollo' (cream and yellow) and *I.* 'Harmony' (royal blue).

Muscari
GRAPE HYACINTH
Hyacinthaceae

H 20cm (8in) **S** 5cm (2in)

Bulbous perennials which produce long, narrow, fleshy leaves and spikes of bell-shaped flowers in spring. They enjoy full sun, and clumps should be divided regularly. *M. armeniacum* bears bright blue flowers, those of its form *M.a.* 'Blue Spike' are double. *M. aucheri* 'Tubergenianum' has blue flowers with a crown of sterile florets, while those of *M. botryoides* 'Album' are white and fragrant.

Narcissus
DAFFODIL
Amaryllidaceae

H 15 – 60cm (6 – 24in)

Bulbous perennials, producing long, strap-like leaves and stems bearing between one and 20 flowers, usually yellow or white, occasionally with red, orange or pink. Of the hundreds of

hybrids, *N.* 'Rip van Winkle' is small, producing double, yellow flowers with pointed petals, *N.* 'St Keverne' is tall, with single, rich golden flowers, and *N.* 'Scarlet Gem' bears clusters of fragrant yellow flowers with orange centres. *N.* 'Peeping Tom' produces dainty flowers.

Primula
Primulaceae

H 20cm (8in)
S 25 – 35cm (10 – 14in)

Many species and hybrid primulas flower in spring, giving a colourful display of red, orange, yellow, white, pink or purple. They are tolerant of sun or partial shade, but need a moist soil. *P. vulgaris* (primrose) is a rosette-forming perennial, with single flowers on short stems. In the wild these are pale yellow, but cultivated forms are available in many colours: *P.v.* 'Jack in the Green' has yellow flowers backed by green bracts; *P.v.* subsp. *sibthorpii* has rose-pink, red, white or purple flowers. *P. auricula* produces clusters of fragrant, deep yellow flowers on a tall stem. Other forms have red or purple flowers

Erysimum 'Bowles Mauve'

Crocus × *luteus* 'Dutch Yellow'

Muscari armeniacum

with a yellow centre, such as *P.a.* 'Mark' (wine-red and yellow), and *P.a.* 'Adrian' (purple-blue and pale yellow).

Rhododendron (and Azalea)
Ericaceae

H 1 – 4m (3 – 12ft)

Preferring acid soil, rhododendrons and azaleas flower throughout spring, from early *R.* 'Praecox' (rose-purple), to dwarf mid-season azaleas such as *R.* 'Hino-mayo' (pink flowers), and the superb *R. yakushimanum* (rich pink in bud, opening paler and fading to white, with cinnamon-coloured down on the leaves). Flower colours include shades of white, pink, orange, red, purple and yellow, and preference for sun or partial shade varies between species.

Scilla siberica
SIBERIAN SQUILL
Hyacinthaceae

H 10 – 20cm (4 – 8in)
S 5cm (2in)

A delicate-looking (but quite hardy), bulbous perennial with long, slender leaves and bright blue, wide bell- or bowl-shaped

Narcissus 'Peeping Tom'

Scilla siberica

flowers carried in clusters of 4-5 on dark green stems. *S.s.* 'Alba' has white flowers, *S.s.* 'Spring Beauty' has deep blue flowers. Grow in full sun or partial shade, and allow to dry during summer dormancy.

Tulipa
TULIP
Liliaceae

H 20 – 60cm (8 – 24in)
S 15 – 20cm (6 – 8in)

Bulbous perennials which vary widely in leaf and flower colour, shape and size. Flowers are generally cup-shaped with six overlapping petals, and may be borne singly or in clusters of up to 12. *T. fosteriana* and hybrids have single bowl-shaped flowers, white, yellow or red, sometimes with a contrasting-coloured base and margins. The leaves are often marked with red-purple. *T. purissima*, formerly *T.* 'White Emperor', in the Fosteriana group, has pure white flowers. In the Greigii group, *T.* 'Red Riding Hood' has bright scarlet flowers and maroon-marked leaves. *T. kaufmanniana* (water-lily tulip) has wide-spreading cream-yellow flowers flushed pink, orange or red outside. *T. praestans* bears clusters of up to five orange-red flowers. *T. clusiana* has white flowers, striped pink on the outside. Prefers full sun and shelter.

Viola
VIOLET
Violaceae

H 10cm (4in)

Low-growing perennials with heart-shaped leaves and dainty flowers, which will grow in full sun or partial shade. *V. canina* (wild violet) has blue, violet or white flowers. *V. cornuta* has violet-blue flowers with white markings. *V. labradorica* has bronze-purple young foliage and purple flowers. *V. tricolor* (heartsease) self-seeds freely and produces flowers from spring to autumn which combine purple, lavender, white and yellow tints. *V. bicolor* is a dwarf, creeping perennial with yellow flowers.

SUMMER

Ageratum houstonianum
FLOSS FLOWER

Compositae

H and **S** 15 – 30cm (6 – 12in)

Butterflies love the long-lasting, fluffy-looking flowerheads of ageratum, in their shades of blue, pink and white. Tolerant of slightly dry conditions, grow them in a sunny, sheltered position, perhaps as edging plants. *A.h.* 'Bavaria' has blue and white flowers, *A.h.* 'Hawaii White' has white flowers, *A.h.* 'Pacific' are a deep violet-blue, and those of *A.h.* 'Swing Pink' are bright candy-pink. *A.h.* 'Blue Danube' produces numerous lavender-blue flowers.

Armeria
SEA PINK, THRIFT

Plumbaginaceae

H 30 – 50cm (12 – 20in)

S 25 – 30cm (10 – 12in)

Hardy, tolerant plants which thrive in full sun in any soil, as long as it is well-drained. Good edging plants, they are cushion-forming, with slender, strap-like leaves, and flowers carried in rounded heads during late spring to early summer. *A. juniperifolia* has purple-pink to white flowers. *A. maritima* has red-purple, pink or white flowers, the form 'Bloodstone' has dark red flowers, and 'Vindictive' has rosy-pink flowers.

Bellis perennis
DAISY

Compositae

H and **S** 5 – 20cm (2 – 8in)

A rosette-forming perennial with bright green, rounded leaves, which will grow in most situations, and will seed itself readily unless regularly dead-headed. It produces red, pink or white flowers with yellow centres throughout spring and summer. The Pomponette Series has double flowers up to 4cm (1.5in) across, and the Tasso Series has double flowers up to 6cm (2.5in) across.

Calendula officinalis
MARIGOLD

Compositae

H 30 – 60cm (12 – 24in)

S 30 – 45cm (12 – 18in)

Hardy annuals which self-seed readily, and thrive in full sun and poor soil. Single or double daisy-like flowers, up to 10cm (4in) across, are produced all summer, in shades of orange, yellow and cream with a purple or brown centre. *C.o.* 'Fiesta Gitana' is dwarf, with double, pale yellow or orange flowers. *C.o.* 'Indian Prince' has brown-tinted, dark orange flowers.

Dianthus
PINK

Caryophyllaceae

H 25 – 45cm (10 – 18in)

S 40cm (16in)

Evergreen, mound-forming perennials which prefer alkaline conditions in full sun. Flowers are single, semi-double or double, with up to six blooms per stem, and of many colour combinations. *D.* 'Gran's Favourite' has clove-scented white flowers with mauve edgings and centres. *D.* 'Doris' has fragrant, double flowers of pale pink with darker centres. *D.* 'Mrs Sinkins' has fragrant, double, fringed white flowers.

Dictamnus albus
BURNING BUSH

Rutaceae

H 40 – 90cm (16 – 36in)

S 60cm (24in)

A clump-forming perennial with divided, lemon-scented leaves. Tall, loose spikes of white or pink-tinted flowers with long stamens are produced in early summer. Grows well in any soil, and in full sun or partial shade. *D.a. var. purpureus* has mauve flowers with darker veins.

Gazania
Compositae

H 20 – 25cm (8 – 10in)

S 25cm (10in)

Annuals or half-hardy perennials with hairy, grey-green leaves. The large, daisy-like flowers

Ageratum houstonianum 'Blue Danube'

come in shades of red, orange, yellow and white. They enjoy well-drained soil and full sun, and are ideal for containers. G. Chansonette Series is perennial, bearing flowers with a darker central ring. G. Daybreak Series has glossy foliage, G. Mini-star Series is compact, and G. Talent Series is vigorous.

Geranium
CRANESBILL

Geraniaceae

H 15 – 60cm (6 – 24in)

S 30 – 90cm (12 – 36in)

Versatile, tolerant, hardy plants which will grow in almost any situation. The widely varying flowers are in shades of purple, blue, pink or white. *G. cinereum* is a dwarf, rosette-forming perennial with white or pink purple-veined flowers. *G. himalayense* 'Gravetye' has blue flowers with a white centre surrounded by purple-red. Low-growing *G. sanguineum* bears magenta flowers all summer, *G.s.* 'Album' is pure white. G. Johnson's Blue' has lavender-blue flowers with pink-tinged centres.

Gladiolus
Iridaceae

H 0.45 – 1.7m (1.5 – 5.5ft)

S 5 – 15cm (2 – 6in)

Upright, sun-loving, perennials that grow from a corm to produce a spike of funnel-shaped flowers, opening from the base upwards. Plant in groups for impact. *G. callianthus* produces fragrant, white flowers with purple-red centres in late summer. *G. cardinalis* bears red

Ageratum houstonianum 'Blue Danube'

Armeria maritima

Bellis perennis

flowers with white markings, G. 'Christabel' has yellow flowers with purple markings, and *G. byzantinus* produces magenta flowers in early summer.

Impatiens
BUSY LIZZIE

Balsaminaceae

H and **S** 30cm (12in)

Reliable and tolerant, the busy Lizzie will flower throughout the summer, preferring shelter, partial shade and moist conditions. *I. balsamina* is a slightly hairy, bushy plant bearing red, pink, purple or white flowers – the Tom Thumb group are dwarf with large, double flowers. *I.* New Guinea Hybrids have gold-splashed, bronze or green foliage and bearing purple, red, salmon, pink or white flowers.

Lychnis
CAMPION

Caryophyllaceae

H 15 – 120cm (6 – 48in)

S 15 – 45cm (6 – 18in)

Ranging from the dwarf to the tall, with flower colours

Calendula officinalis

Dictamnus albus

Geranium 'Johnson's Blue'

Nicotiana × *sanderae*

Gazania 'Tiger'

Impatiens hybrid

including red, pink and white, Lychnis are varied and tolerant perennials. *L.* × *arkwrightii* 'Vesuvius' bears bright scarlet flowers amid bronze foliage. *L. chalcedonica* has rounded clusters of red flowers, while *L. coronaria* is widely branched, with woolly-grey leaves and magenta or white flowers. *L. flosjovis* is mat-forming, with pink, white or scarlet flowers.

Nepeta
CATMINT
Labiatae
H 45 – 90cm (18 – 36in)
S 45 – 60cm (18 – 24in)

These clump-forming perennials enjoy well-drained soil in full sun or partial shade. Two-lipped flowers are borne in spikes, in shades of white, blue and purple. *N.* × *faassenii* has silvery, aromatic leaves and pale lavender flowers. *N. sibirica* is upright and leafy, with blue flowers. *N.* 'Six Hills Giant' is hardy and vigorous, with blue flowers. *N.* 'Souvenir d'André Chaudron' is smaller, with darker flowers.

Nicotiana
TOBACCO PLANT
Solanaceae
H 23 – 60cm (9 – 24in)
S 25 – 35cm (10 – 14in)

Half-hardy annuals bearing trumpet-shaped flowers. Grow in full sun. *N.* × *sanderae* is an upright annual with open panicles of flowers in shades of red, pink, purple or white. Domino Series has upward-facing flowers in combinations of red, pink, white, lime-green and purple. Havana Series

plants are compact, and the Merlin Series is ideal for containers as it is dwarf.

Osteospermum
Compositae
H and S 45 – 60cm (18 – 24in)

Evergreen subshrubs or perennials, grown for their large, daisy-like flowers of yellow, pink, purple or white, often with darker centres. *O.* 'Buttermilk' is upright, with butter-yellow petals, flushed white at the centre and edged bronze. *O. jucundum* has grey-green leaves and magenta flowers with purple centres which age to gold. *O.* 'Whirligig' has crimped white petals which are blue beneath, with a purple-blue centre.

Pelargonium
GERANIUM
Geraniaceae
H 20 – 45cm (8 – 18in)
S 15 – 30cm (6 – 12in)

A huge group of plants which are generally half-hardy, flower profusely all summer, and are ideal as bedding or in containers, especially hanging baskets. Of

the upright pelargoniums – Regal, Zonal, Scented-leaved and Unique – *P.* 'Lord Bute' (Regal) has clusters of dark reddish-black flowers, *P.* 'Sefton' (Regal) has cerise and deep red flowers; *P.* 'Ann Hoysted' (Zonal) has deep red flowers; *P.* 'Mabel Grey' (Scented-leaved) has strongly lemon-scented leaves and mauve flowers; while *P.* 'Voodoo' (Unique) bears clusters of wine-red flowers with purple-black markings. (See also page 128, TRAILING PLANTS).

Rosa
MINIATURE & PATIO ROSES
Rosaceae
H 15 – 60cm (6 – 24in)
S 30cm (12in)

A group of small, bushy roses which produce masses of small, double flowers throughout summer and autumn. They are ideal in containers or small borders and as edging, in sunny positions. Patio roses are also available as short standards on stems up to 90cm (36in). *R.* 'Baby Masquerade' has double, yellow-pink flowers, *R.* 'Darling

Flame' has double, orange-red flowers, and *R.* 'Top Gear' has red flowers with white markings.

Rudbeckia
CONEFLOWER
Compositae
H 60 – 90cm (24 – 36in)
S 45 – 90cm (18 – 36in)

Annuals, biennials and perennials which enjoy moist soil in full sun or partial shade. Daisy-like flowers in shades of yellow, orange and red are produced through summer and autumn. *R. fulgida* has yellow flowers with dark brown centres; *var. deamii* and *var. sullivantii* 'Goldsturm' are both shorter, the latter having large, golden-yellow flowers. *R. hirta* is biennial, with forms including 'Kelvedon Star', 'Marmalade' and 'Rustic Dwarfs'.

Salvia
SAGE
Labiatae
H 40 – 90cm (16 – 36in)
S 30 – 60cm (12 – 24in)

A widely varied group of frost- and fully hardy plants. Two-lipped flowers are borne on spikes, and foliage is often aromatic. *S. greggii* (autumn sage) is a dwarf evergreen shrub with pairs of purple, red, pink, yellow or violet flowers, *S.g.* 'Raspberry Royal' has raspberry-coloured flowers. *S. patens* is a tuberous perennial with deep blue flowers, while *S.p.* 'Cambridge Blue' is paler.

AUTUMN & WINTER

Chrysanthemum
Compositae

H 60 – 75cm (24 – 30in)
s 30cm (12in)

Bushy annuals and herbaceous perennials, grown for their showy, fragrant flowers in late summer and autumn. Grow in full sun in a well-drained soil. *C. carinatum* is an upright annual with daisy-like flowers of yellow or white with purple centres. *C.c.* 'Court Jesters' bear flowers of white, yellow, orange, red and maroon, zoned with red or orange. *C.* 'Mary Stoker' has single, apricot-yellow flowers.

Cyclamen
SOWBREAD
Primulaceae

H 5 – 12cm (2 – 5in)
s 10 – 15cm (4 – 6in)

Tuberous perennials which need a warm, dry summer dormancy, so are ideal for the rock garden, raised bed or container. *C. cilicium* has white or pink flowers in autumn. *C. coum* has rounded leaves, plain deep green or patterned with silver-green, and nodding flowers with reflexed petals in shades of pink and carmine-red in winter. *C. hederifolium* flowers in mid- to late autumn, in shades of pink.

Daphne bholua
Thymelaeceae

H 2 – 4m (6 – 12ft) s 1.5m (5ft)

An upright shrub with leathery, oval-shaped, dark green leaves. Prefers cool, moist roots and slightly alkaline soil, and full sun or partial shade. The heavily fragrant, white-flushed pink flowers are produced in clusters at the ends of the shoots in winter, followed by round, purple-black fruits. *D.b.* 'Gurkha' is deciduous and very hardy, *D.b.* 'Jacqueline Postill' is evergreen with large flowers, white inside, purple-pink outside.

Gaultheria (Pernettya)
Ericaceae

H to 1m (3ft) s to 1.5m (5ft)

Hardy, evergreen shrubs with small, oval, pointed, glossy dark green leaves on slender red stems. Flowers in late spring are followed in autumn by clusters of long-lasting bright, round fruits. *G. mucronata* has varieties with berries in red and pale lilac; others are white, pink, purple or blue.

Hamamelis
WITCH HAZEL
Hamamelidaceae

H and s 4m (12ft)

Hardy shrubs preferring neutral to acid soil and shelter, bearing small, fragrant, spidery flowers during winter, and having wonderful autumn leaf colours. *H. × intermedia* bears yellow, orange or red flowers, its form 'Diane' has dark-red flowers, and 'Jelena' has copper-orange flowers (both have fiery autumn foliage). *H. mollis* has golden-yellow flowers – its form 'Sandra' has purple young foliage, good autumn tints, and dark yellow flowers.

Iris unguicularis
Iridaceae

H up to 30cm (12in)
s 10cm (4in)

A vigorous, rhizomatous iris, bearing large, fragrant pale- to deep-purple flowers with yellow markings on short stems. They appear in late winter and early spring. *I.u.* 'Alba' has white flowers with yellow markings. *I.u.* 'Mary Barnard' has bright violet flowers in midwinter. Grow in full sun in a well-drained, neutral to alkaline soil, preferably with some shelter.

Mahonia
Berberidaceae

H and s 1 – 4m (3 – 12ft)

Hardy shrubs, preferring full or partial shade, with prickly, leathery, pinnate leaves and spikes of bright yellow, sweetly scented flowers in winter. *M. aquifolium* has bright green leaves which turn reddish in winter as the dense flower clusters appear, followed by blue-black berries. *M. × media* (including forms such as *M. × m.* 'Charity' and 'Winter Sun') is upright and taller, with longer racemes of flowers.

Schizostylis coccinea
KAFFIR LILY
Iridaceae

H 60cm (24in) s 30cm (12in)

Flowering from late summer to early winter, these evergreen rhizomatous perennials are grown for their tall spikes of gladiolus-like, cup-shaped flowers in shades of red, pink, magenta and white. They are excellent in containers and as cut flowers. Later-flowering forms include *S.c. var. alba* (white flowers), *S.c.* 'Major' (large red flowers) and *S.c.* 'Sunrise' (large, salmon-pink flowers).

Skimmia japonica
Rutaceae

H and s 1m (39in)

A compact shrub with oval-shaped, slightly aromatic leaves, preferring partial shade. *S.j.* 'Rubella' is a male clone with red edges to the leaves, and panicles of dark-red flower buds which form in autumn and winter, and open in late winter and early spring. A female clone, such as *S.j.* 'Rogersii', planted nearby will form clusters of red berries which last until the next flush of flowers.

Viola × wittrockiana
PANSY
Violaceae

H 15 – 23cm (6 – 9in)
s 23 – 30cm (9 – 12in)

Hardy new pansy varieties mean that there are some in flower throughout the year, for winter containers and baskets as well as summer ones. *V. × wittrockiana* cultivars include many of the large-flowered, brightly coloured pansies bred to flower during winter. They are tolerant of sun and shade, but need dead-heading to maintain flowering. Flower colours include purple, blue, white, yellow, orange, pink and red, as single or bicoloured, often with central markings of a different colour, including black.

Cyclamen hederifolium

Daphne bholua 'Gurkha'

Iris unguicularis

WATER & DAMP

Many patio gardens are large enough to include a tiny pond, and a simple pool can be created quite easily even from a container (see pages 102-3). Having a small water feature allows you to grow a wider range of plants, and adds interest to the planting as a consequence. Not all plants enjoy wet conditions; many are happier in bog-like soil, which can be created next to a water feature by simply sinking a plastic liner, pierced to make it permeable, a spit or so beneath the soil's surface.

Caltha palustris 'Flore Pleno'

Ligularia dentata 'Desdemona'

Aponogeton distachyos
WATER HAWTHORN
Aponogetonaceae
H 10 – 15cm (4 – 6in)
S 1.2m (4ft)

A frost-hardy aquatic perennial with bright green, long, oval leaves which float on the water surface from a submerged rhizome. Clusters of small, white, hawthorn-scented flowers are carried just above the water in spring and autumn. Grow in soil or planting baskets in water 1m (3ft) deep, preferably in full sun. Remove dead flowers and foliage from the water.

Caltha palustris
MARSH MARIGOLD
Ranunculaceae
H 10 – 40cm (4 – 16in)
S 45cm (18in)

A marginal perennial with dark green, kidney-shaped leaves and cup-shaped yellow or white flowers in spring and an occasional second flush in summer. Grow in very moist soil or a partially submerged planting basket, preferably in full sun. *C.p. var. alba* is compact with yellow-centred white flowers in early spring. *C.p.* 'Flore Pleno' has double yellow flowers.

Iris
WATER IRIS
Iridaceae
H 80cm (32in)

Hardy perennials with purple, blue, pink, red, yellow or white flowers which enjoy slightly acidic marginal conditions in wet or very moist soil. *I. kaempferi* (*I. ensata*) has red-purple flowers, the form 'Blue Peter' has bright blue flowers, and 'Moonlight Waves' has white flowers with green centres. *I. laevigata* has purple-blue flowers, the form 'Rosea' has pink flowers, and 'Variegata' has green- and white-striped foliage. (See pages 131 and 134, SEASONAL COLOUR: SPRING and AUTUMN & WINTER).

Lagarosiphon major (formerly Elodea crispa)
CURLY WATER THYME
Hydrocharitaceae
H up to 1m (3ft) **S** indefinite

A submerged, hardy aquatic perennial with stems up to 1m (3ft) long, branching, and covered with curved, dark green leaves. Acts as an oxygenator, gradually forming a dense mass which will need reducing – not difficult, as the stems are easily broken. Remove all debris from the water. Tiny greenish-pink flowers appear among the leaves in summer.

Ligularia dentata
Compositae
H 1 – 1.5m (3 – 5ft) **S** 1m (3ft)

A hardy perennial which needs a constantly moist (but not wet) soil and full sun, and benefits from some shelter. It has rounded leaves with red-tinted lower leaf stalks, and upright spikes of daisy-like flowers in yellow or orange with brown centres, produced during summer and autumn.
L.d. 'Desdemona' has brownish leaves, purple beneath, and deep orange flowers.

Nymphaea
WATER LILY (miniature)
Nymphaeaceae
S 75 – 90cm (30 – 36in)

Herbaceous perennials with round, floating leaves and showy, sometimes scented, flowers in shades of red, pink, white, yellow and blue. Choose small varieties, and grow in full sun. *N.* 'Albida' has red-tinted leaves and white flowers. *N.* 'Ellisiana' has dark green leaves and red flowers with orange stamens. The flowers of *N.* 'Indiana' are apricot, turning to dark orange-red, with orange stamens.

Pontederia cordata
PICKEREL WEED
Pontederiaceae
H 90 – 120cm (3 – 4ft)
S 60 – 75cm (24 – 30in)

A fully hardy marginal perennial which prefers to grow in full sun, and in no more than 10cm (4in) of water. Bright green, lance-shaped foliage may rise above, lie on or remain below the surface of the water. Upright spikes of tubular, two-lipped, blue flowers are produced in late summer. *P.c. var. lancefolia* is taller, and has longer, narrower leaves.

Primula denticulata
DRUMSTICK PRIMULA
Primulaceae
H and **S** 45cm (18in)

A hardy, rosette-forming, deciduous perennial with long, rounded, mid-green leaves, whitish beneath. Prefers a neutral to acid soil which is

Pontederia cordata

constantly moist (but not wet), in full sun or partial shade. Robust, upright stems carry spherical clusters of tightly packed trumpet-shaped flowers of purple with a yellow centre from spring to summer. *P. d. alba* has white flowers, and those of the variety 'Rubra' are reddish-purple.

Rodgersia pinnata
Saxifragaceae
H 1.2m (4ft) **S** 75cm (30in)

A clump-forming, rhizomatous perennial which prefers to grow in a constantly moist soil, in full sun or partial shade, sheltered from cold winds. Leaves are divided, on long reddish-green stems, and so heavily veined that they appear crinkled. Loose spikes of small, star-shaped flowers are produced in summer, in shades of creamy-white, pink or red. *R.p.* 'Superba' has bronze-purple young leaves and bright pink flowers.

HERBS & EDIBLE PLANTS

Lavandula angustifolia

Most gardeners, with only a tiny area in which to garden, hanker after a few plants that can be plucked and eaten fresh. Herbs are the ideal candidates for sunny situations, such as windowsills, and many of them can be grown very successfully from seed in small containers. With just a little more space, you could create a tiny herb garden, neatly edged in clipped box, each section filled with a favourite herb.

You can grow herbs for their medicinal properties or their culinary value, or simply because you like the look of them. Their gentle colours and frequently aromatic scent have a wonderfully soothing effect, and many, like lavender or marjoram, for example, attract bees or butterflies.

A few edible plants, notably lettuces, tomatoes, strawberries, beans and potatoes, do well in containers, whether humble plastic growing bags, disguised with a simple wooden surround, or more elaborate specially constructed planters (those for potatoes and strawberries in terracotta have planting holes incorporated up the sides of the pot). Edible plants, to survive, need a rich soil and plenty of water, as well as sunshine to ripen the crops in the case of strawberries and tomatoes. Tomatoes, in particular, need sun, copious watering and plenty of fertilizer if they are to produce worthwhile crops. They will need supporting on canes. Runner beans require similar feeding and watering. They can be staked on a cane wigwam (see pages 18-9), looking highly ornamental as well as offering a good crop of beans throughout the late summer months. Lettuces grow very easily from seed and the oak-leaved forms are sufficiently attractive to be used as edging to a small bed.

HERBS

Allium schoenoprasum
CHIVES
Alliaceae
H 30 – 60cm (12 – 24in)
s 10 – 15cm (4 – 6in)
A hardy, bulbous, clump-forming perennial grown for its edible, hollow, dark green leaves, which have a mild onion flavour. Grow in well-drained soil, preferably in full sun. Dense, round heads of purple (or occasionally white) flowers appear in summer. The flowers of *A.s.* 'Forescate' are deep pink.

Anthriscus cerefolium
CHERVIL
Umbelliferae
H 50 – 60cm (20 – 24in)
s 30cm (12in)
A hardy, upright annual with finely divided, aniseed-flavoured leaves. Grows in full sun or partial shade in any well-drained soil, but watering must be maintained during drought, or it will bolt. Produces umbels of tiny white flowers in summer.

Lavandula angustifolia 'Hidcote'
LAVENDER
Labiatae
H 60cm (24in) s 75cm (30in)
A compact, hardy shrub which likes full sun and a well-drained

soil, but looks good in a container, at the front of a border or as a low-growing hedge. It has silvery leaves and fragrant, dark purple flowers during summer, which may be picked and dried for use indoors in potpourri or among clothes to deter moths.

Mentha
MINT
Labiatae
H 10 – 90cm (4 – 36in)
s 50cm (20in) – indefinite
Hardy, rhizomatous perennials which will spread indefinitely if the roots are not restricted. Grow in any moist soil, in full sun, but restrict by planting in containers, or pots plunged into the soil. Forms include:
M. × *gracilis* 'Variegata' (ginger mint); M. × *piperita citrata* (eau-de-Cologne mint); M. *pulegium* (pennyroyal); M. *requienii* (Corsican mint); M. *spicata* (spearmint); M. *suaveolens* (apple mint); and M. × *villosa alopecuroides* (Bowles' mint).

Ocimum basilicum
BASIL
Labiatae
H 30 – 60cm (12 – 24in)
s 30cm (12in)
Usually grown as a half-hardy annual, basil will need a warm,

Lavandula angustifolia 'Hidcote'

Mentha × *piperita*

sheltered position and a constant supply of water, in a well-drained soil or compost. The bright green, pointed-oval leaves are delicious when cooked with tomato dishes. Spikes of pinkish, two-lipped flowers are produced in summer. *O.b.* 'Dark Opal' has dark red-purple leaves, and *O.b. minimum* is more compact.

Origanum vulgare
MARJORAM, OREGANO
Labiatae
H and **S** 30 – 60cm (12 – 24in)

A woody, bush-forming perennial with aromatic oval leaves which are used as flavouring for meat, soups etc. Enjoys growing in full sun, in a well-drained and preferably alkaline soil. Loose heads of small flowers are produced during summer, from pale to dark pink, or white. The form 'Aureum' has golden-yellow foliage, 'Compactum' is smaller and dome-shaped, and 'Variegatum' has yellow tips to the leaves.

Petroselinum crispum
PARSLEY
Umbelliferae
H 60 – 80cm (24 – 32in)
S 60cm (24in)

A hardy biennial more often grown as an annual, with bright green, edible foliage used in cooking or as a garnish. Grow in well-drained soil in full sun or partial shade. Forms include

Salvia officinalis 'Purpurascens'

P.c. 'Afro' (upright, with tightly curled leaves), 'Clivi' (compact), *neapolitanum* (Italian parsley, has flatter leaves and a stronger flavour), and *var. tuberosum* (Hamburg parsley, which has edible roots).

Rosmarinus officinalis
ROSEMARY
Labiatae
H and **S** 1 – 1.5m (3 – 5ft)

A hardy, evergreen shrub with aromatic foliage and small two-lipped flowers in blue, purple or white from late spring through to autumn. Grow in full sun in a well-drained soil or compost, individually or as a hedge. Forms include 'Aureus' (yellow variegated leaves), 'Miss Jessopp's Upright' (erect-growing, but vigorous with blue flowers), 'Prostratus' (low, trailing stems, but not so hardy), and 'Roseus' (pink flowers).

Salvia officinalis
SAGE
Labiatae
H 60 – 80cm (24 – 32in)
S 60 – 90cm (24 – 36in)

A woody, evergreen perennial with long, oval, aromatic leaves, used in such dishes as stuffings and sausages. Small, purple-blue flowers are produced in summer. Prefers moist, but well-drained soil in full sun or light shade, and will thrive in a container. Forms include 'Icterina' (variegated yellow and green leaves), 'Purpurascens' (reddish-purple leaves), and 'Tricolor' (creamy white variegations on grey-green leaves, young foliage also flushed pink).

EDIBLE PLANTS

Fragaria vesca
STRAWBERRY
Rosaceae
H 10 – 15cm (4 – 6in)
S indefinite

Ideal plants for growing in containers, as their habit of spreading by runners means that they can get out of control in the garden. Grow in full sun or very light shade in moist, but

Lycopersicon esculentum 'Phyra'

well-drained soil or compost. White flowers appear from early summer until autumn, depending on variety, followed by the sweet red fruits. Cut runners off as they appear or root new plants by pegging into pots of compost.

Lactuca sativa
LETTUCE
Compositae
H 25cm (10in)
S up to 30cm (12in)

The three main types – cabbage, leaf and Cos – can all be grown in containers or soil, as long as they are well-fed and given sufficient water. They prefer full sun. Leaf varieties such as 'Lollo Blonda', 'Lollo Rossa' and 'Salad Bowl' do not form a heart as such, so leaves can be removed on a cut-and-come-again basis. The small Cos types 'Bubbles' and 'Little Gem' are ideal for the smaller garden.

Lycopersicon esculentum
TOMATO
Solanaceae
H up to 1.2m (4ft)
S up to 60cm (24in)

Tomatoes may be grown in the ground, in growing bags or in containers, under cover or outdoors (depending on the variety). Outdoors, the crop will depend on the weather, but varieties such as *L.e.* 'Gardener's Delight' or 'Phyra' are usually reliable choices. 'Tumbler' and

'Tiny Tim' are ideal for plant pots, windowboxes and hanging baskets.

Phaseolus
RUNNER BEAN, FRENCH BEAN
Leguminosae
H up to 1.2m (4ft) **S** 60cm (24in)

Dwarf varieties of both runner and French beans are suitable for growing in small gardens, either in the ground or in containers. Sow in late spring and grow in a sunny position, staking if necessary. Dwarf runner varieties include 'Hammond's Dwarf Scarlet' and 'Pickwick'. Dwarf French varieties include 'Annabel', 'Forum', 'Masai' and 'Vibel'.

Solanum tuberosum
POTATO
Solanaceae
H and **S** 60 – 90cm (24 – 36in)

Potatoes will grow in any container (even in a strong black bin-liner) which is at least 30cm (12in) wide and deep with drainage holes in the base, and standing in a sunny position. Lay 2–3 chitted potatoes on 10 – 12cm (4 – 5in) of compost/soil in the container and cover with a similar depth of compost/soil. Cover with another similar depth once the shoots are about 15cm (6in) tall, leaving the tips showing. Repeat until the shoots are within 5cm (2in) of the rim.

PLANT LISTS

A selection of plants (the majority of which are detailed in the Plant Finder on pages 120–137) for particular purposes or situations is given on these pages. The listing includes not only the best container and hanging basket plants, but also a few small trees and evergreen shrubs to give structure to the planting. Each plant is categorized according to type – tree, shrub, perennial, etc. There is also a selection of plants for flower colour and foliage colour.

KEY
a = annual and biennial
a/p = tender perennials treated
   as annuals
b = bulb
c = climber
p = perennial
s = shrub
t = tree

Container plants

Agapanthus (p – blue)
Ageratum (a – blue)
Alonsoa (a – orange)
Argyranthemum (a/p – white,
   pink, yellow)
Begonia semperflorens (a – mixed
   colours)
Begonia x tuberhybrida (a/p –
   pink, red, orange, white)
Bidens ferulifolia (a – yellow)
Brachyscome iberidifolia (a –
   blue)
Buxus sempervirens (s – foliage)
Cordyline australis (p – foliage)
Diascia (p – pink, orange)
Felicia amelloides (a – blue)
Fuchsia (s – pink, purple, red)
Helichrysum petiolare (a/p –
   foliage)
Hosta (p – foliage)
Hyacinthus (b – mixed colours)
Hydrangea (s – blue, pink,
   white)
Impatiens walleriana (a/p – white,
   pink, red)
Laurus nobilis (s – foliage)
Lobelia (a – blue, pink, white)
Narcissus (b – yellow, white)
Nemisia (a – mixed colours)
Pelargonium (a/p – orange, pink,
   red, white)
Petunia (a/p – mixed colours)
Phormium (p – foliage)
Primula (p – mixed colours)
Senecio cineraria (a/p – foliage)
Tagetes (a – yellow, orange)
Tropaeolum (a – red, orange,
   yellow)
Tulipa (b – mixed colours)
Verbena x hybrida (a/p – mixed
   colours)
Viola x wittrockiana (a – mixed
   colours)

Hanging basket plants

Ageratum (a – blue)
Alonsoa (a – orange)
Argyranthemum (a/p – white,
   pink, yellow)
Begonia semperflorens (a – mixed
   colours)
Begonia x tuberhybrida (a/p –
   pink, red, orange, white)
Bidens ferulifolia (a – yellow)
Brachyscome iberidifolia (a –
   blue)
Diascia (p – pink, orange)
Felicia amelloides (a – blue)
Fuchsia (s – pink, purple, red)
Glechoma hederacea ‘Variegata’
   (a – foliage)
Hedera helix (p – foliage)
Helichrysum petiolare (a/p –
   foliage)
Impatiens walleriana (a – white,
   pink, red)
Lobelia erinus (a – blue, pink,
   white)
Lotus berthelottii (p – orange,
   foliage)
Narcissus (b – yellow, white)
Pelargonium (a/p – orange, pink,
   red, white)
Petunia (a/p – mixed colours)
Plectranthus coleoides (a/p –
   foliage)
Primula (p – mixed colours)
Scaevola (a/p – purple, blue)
Senecio cinerea (a/p – foliage)
Tagetes (a – yellow, orange)
Tropaeolum (a – red, orange,
   yellow)
Tulipa (b – mixed colours)
Verbena x hybrida (a/p – mixed
   colours)
Viola x wittrockiana (a – mixed
   colours)

Plants for colour

Blue/mauve flowers
Agapanthus spp. and cvs. (p)
Ageratum spp. and cvs. (a)
Ajuga reptans (p)
Aquilegia flabellata (p)
Aster amellus (p)
Brunnera macrophylla (p)
Campanula spp. and cvs. (p)

Caryopteris x clandonensis (s)
Catananche caerulea (p)
Ceanothus spp. and cvs. (s)
Clematis cvs. (c)
Delphinium spp. and cvs. (p)
Echinops ritro (p)
Gentiana spp. and cvs. (p)
Geranium spp. and cvs. (p)
Hebe spp. and cvs. (s)
Hosta spp. and cvs. (p)
Hyacinthoides hispanica (b)
Hydrangea spp. and cvs. (s)
Iris spp. and cvs. (p)
Lavandula angustifolia (s)
Meconopsis spp. (p)
Muscari spp. and cvs. (b)
Nepeta spp. and cvs. (p)
Nigella damascena (a)
Omphalodes cappadocica (p)
Penstemon heterophyllus (p)
Perovskia atriplicifolia (s)
Plumbago spp. (s)
Polemonium caeruleum (p)
Primula spp. and cvs. (p)
Pulmonaria spp. and cvs. (p)
Salvia spp. and cvs. (p & s)
Scabiosa caucasica (p)
Veronica spp. and cvs. (p)
Viola spp. and cvs. (p & a)

Yellow, gold and orange flowers
Achillea spp. and cvs. (p)
Anthemis tinctoria (p)
Aurinia saxatilis (p)
Buphthalmum salicifolium (p)
Clematis tangutica (p)
Coreopsis verticillata (p)
Coronilla valentina (s)
Crocus cvs. (b)
Cytisus x praecox cvs. (s)
Digitalis lutea (p)
Euphorbia spp. and cvs. (p)
Geum ‘Lady Strathenden’ (p)
Helenium spp. and cvs. (p)
Heliopsis spp. and cvs. (p)
Hemerocallis spp. and cvs. (p)
Inula spp. and cvs. (p)
Jasminum nudiflorum (s)
Limnanthes douglasii (a)
Lysimachia nummularia ‘Aurea’
   (p)
Mahonia aquifolium (s)
Narcissus cvs. (b)
Paeonia mlokosewitschii (p)

Primula spp. and cvs. (p)
Rosa cvs. (s & c)
Rudbeckia spp. and cvs. (a & p)
Solidago spp. and cvs. (p)
Tagetes cvs. (a)
Trollius spp. and cvs. (p)
Tropaeolum majus (a)
Tulipa cvs. (b)
Verbascum spp. and cvs. (p)
Viola x wittrockiana (a)

Red flowers
Achillea ‘Cerise Queen’ (p)
Alcea rosea (p)
Astilbe ‘Fanal’ (p)
Centranthus ruber (p)
Cosmos atrosanguineus (p)
Dianthus ‘Brympton Red’ (p)
Fuchsia cvs. (s)
Geum ‘Mrs Bradshaw’ (p)
Impatiens cvs. (a)
Lobelia ‘Cherry Ripe’ (p)
Lupinus ‘Inverewe Red’ (p)
Lychnis chalcedonica (p)
Paeonia spp. and cvs.
Papaver orientale (p)
Pelargonium cvs. (a)
Penstemon ‘Cherry Ripe’ (p)
Petunia cvs. (a)
Potentilla ‘Gibson’s Scarlet’ (p)
Potentilla ‘Red Ace’ (s)
Rosa cvs. (c &s)
Tulipa cvs. (b)

Pink flowers
Anemone x hybrida (p)
Antirrhinum cvs. (a)
Armeria spp. and cvs. (p)
Aster spp. and cvs. (p)
Cistus spp. and cvs. (s)
Colchicum spp. (b)
Cyclamen hederifolium (b)
Dahlia cvs. (b)
Deutzia spp. and cvs. (s)
Dianthus spp. and cvs. (p)
Diascia spp. and cvs. (p)
Dicentra spp. and cvs. (p)
Erigeron ‘Charity’ (p)
Fuchsia cvs. (s)
Geranium spp. and cvs. (p)
Hydrangea spp. and cvs. (s)
Impatiens cvs. (a)
Lamium roseum (p)

Lychnis flos-jovis (p)
Malva moschata (p)
Papaver orientale 'Cedric Morris' (p)
Penstemon 'Hidcote Pink' (p)
Persicaria spp. and cvs. (p)
Petunia cvs. (a)
Primula spp. and cvs. (p)
Sedum spectabile (p)
Sidalcea spp. and cvs. (p)
Tulipa cvs. (b)

Purple flowers

Aster spp. and cvs. (p)
Centaurea spp. and cvs. (p)
Erigeron 'Dunkelste Aller' (p)
Erysimum 'Bowles Mauve' (p)
Exacum affine (a)
Geranium spp. and cvs. (p)
Hebe spp. and cvs. (s)
Hyacinthus cvs. (b)
Liatris spicata (p)
Linaria purpurea (p)
Lythrum spp. and cvs. (p)
Osteospermum jucundum (p)
Penstemon 'Burgundy' (p)
Petunia cvs. (a)
Salvia hormium (a)
Stachys macrantha (p)
Syringa cvs. (s)
Verbena bonariensis (p)

White flowers

Achillea ptarmica 'The Pearl' (p)
Anemone x *hybrida* 'Honorine Jobert' (p)
Anthemis punctata cupaniana (p)
Argyranthemum frutescens (a/p)
Astilbe 'Irrlicht' (p)
Campanula latiloba alba (p)
Cistus spp. (s)
Convolvulus cneorum (s)
Dianthus 'Haytor White' (p)
Echinops sphaerocephalus (p)
Geranium sanguineum 'Album' (p)
Gypsophila paniculata 'Bristol Fairy' (p)
Iberis amara (a)
Lamium maculatum 'White Nancy' (p)
Leucanthemum 'Everest' (p)
Nicotiana cvs. (a)
Olearia spp. (s)
Osmanthus spp. and cvs. (s)
Osteospermum 'Whirligig' (a/p)
Petunia cvs. (a)
Polygonatum x *hybridum*
Potentilla 'Abbotswood' (s)
Prunus spp. and cvs. (s & t)
Pulmonaria 'Sissinghurst White' (p)
Spiraea 'Bridal Wreath' (s)
Viburnum spp. and cvs. (s)
Yucca spp. (s)

Foliage colour

Silver foliage

Artemisia spp. and cvs. (p)
Cerastium tomentosum (p)
Convolvulus cneorum (s)
Cynara cardunculus (p)
Elaeagnus 'Quicksilver' (s)
Eryngium giganteum (p)
Hebe pinguifolia 'Pagei' (s)
Lavandula angustifolia (s)
Melianthus major (a/p)
Onopordum spp. (a)
Pyrus salicifolia 'Pendula' (t)
Santolina chamaecyparis (p)
Senecio cineraria (a/p)
Stachys byzantina (p)
Tanacetum haradjanii (p)

Purple foliage

Acer palmatum 'Atropurpureum' (t)
Ajuga reptans 'Atropurpurea' (p)
Berberis thunbergii 'Atropurpurea' (s)
Clematis recta 'Purpurea' (p)
Cordyline australis 'Atropurpurea' (p)
Corylus maxima 'Purpurea' (s)
Cotinus coggygria 'Royal Purple' (s)
Dahlia 'Bishop of Llandaff' (p)
Foeniculum vulgare 'Purpureum' (p)
Heuchera micrantha 'Palace Purple' (p)
Lobelia cardinalis (p)
Phormium tenax 'Purpureum' (p)
Prunus cerasifera 'Nigra' (t)
Ricinus communis 'Gibsonii' (a)
Rosa glauca (s)
Salvia officinalis 'Purpurascens' (s)
Sedum maximum atropurpureum (p)
Viola riviniana Purpurea Group (p)
Vitis vinifera 'Purpurea' (c)

Golden foliage

Acer japonicum 'Aurea' (t)
Carex stricta 'Bowles' Golden' (p)
Filipendula ulmaria 'Aurea' (p)
Fuchsia 'Golden Treasure' (s)
Gleditsia triacanthos 'Sunburst' (t)
Hebe armstrongii (s)
Hedera helix 'Buttercup' (c)
Hosta spp. and cvs. (p)
Humulus lupulus 'Aureus' (c)
Ligustrum ovalifolium 'Aureum' (s)
Lonicera nitida 'Baggesen's Gold' (s)
Lysimachia nummularia 'Aurea' (p)
Milium effusum 'Aureum' (p)
Oreganum vulgare 'Aureum' (p)

Philadelphus coronarius 'Aureus' (s)
Physocarpus opulifolius 'Luteus' (s)
Robinia pseudoacacia 'Frisia' (t)
Sambucus racemosa 'Plumosa Aurea' (s)
Tanecetum parthenium 'Aureum' (p)
Taxus baccata 'Aurea' (t)

Blue foliage

Elymus magellanicus (p)
Eucalyptus gunnii (t)
Hosta 'Blue Boy' (p)
Hosta 'Hadspen Blue' (p)
Hosta 'Halcyon' (p)
Hosta sieboldiana 'Elegans' (p)

Variegated foliage

Acer negundo 'Variegatum' (t)
Aktinidia kolomikta (s)
Aquilegia vulgaris 'Woodside' (p)
Aralia elata 'Aureovariegata' (t)
Astrantia major 'Sunningdale Variegated' (p)
Brunnera macrophylla 'Hadspen Cream' (p)
Cornus alba 'Elegantissima' (s)
Cortaderia selloana 'Gold Band' (p)
Elaeagnus pungens 'Maculata' (s)
Eryngium bourgatii (p)
Euonymus fortunei 'Emerald 'n' Gold' (s)
Euphorbia marginata (a)
Fragaria x *ananassa* 'Variegata' (p)
Hakonechloa macra 'Aureola' (p)
Hedera spp. and cvs. (c)
Hosta spp. and cvs. (p)
Ilex spp. and cvs. (t)
Iris pallida 'Variegata' (p)
Lamium maculatum (p)
Lonicera japonica 'Aureo-reticulata' (c)
Miscanthus sinensis 'Zebrinus' (p)
Phalaris arundinacea 'Picta' (p)
Phormium tenax 'Sundowner' (p)
Pleioblastus auricomus (p)
Pulmonaria saccharata (p)
Rhamnus alaternus 'Argenteovariegata' (t)
Salvia officinalis 'Icterina' (s)
Silybum marianum (a)
Sisyrinchium striatum 'Aunt May' (p)
Symphytum x *uplandicum* 'Variegatum' (p)
Tanecetum vulgare 'Silver Lace' (p)
Vinca major 'Variegata' (s)

Small trees

Acer japonicum
Betula pendula 'Youngii'
Cercis siliquastrum
Ilex x *altaclarensis*
Laburnum x *waterei* 'Vossii'
Malus 'Profusion'
Prunus serrula
Pyrus salicifolia 'Pendula'
Sorbus hupehensis

Evergreen shrubs

Abelia spp. and cvs.
Azara spp.
Berberis spp. and cvs.
Buxus sempervirens
Ceanothus ssp. and cvs.
Choisya ternata
Convolvulus cneorum
Cotoneaster spp. and cvs.
Daphne spp. and cvs.
Elaeagnus pungens
Escalonia spp. and cvs.
Euonymus fortunei
Garrya elliptica
Hebe spp. and cvs.
Ilex spp. and cvs.
Laurus nobilis
Mahonia spp. and cvs.
Osmanthus spp. and cvs.
Photinia spp. and cvs.
Pieris spp. and cvs.
Prunus lusitanicus
Rhododendron spp. and cvs.
Sarcococca spp. and cvs.
Skimmia japonica
Viburnum tinus
Vinca spp. and cvs.

GLOSSARY

A

Annual Plant that completes its cycle of germination from setting seed through to dying in a single growing season.

B

Biennial Plant requiring two growing seasons to flower and seed.
Bract Leaf at base of flower stalk or flowerhead; may resemble a small, normal leaf or, in some plants, be large and brightly coloured.
Bulb Plant storage organ, usually formed underground, containing the following year's growth buds.
Bulbil A very small or secondary bulb that forms, e.g. on lilies.

C

Calyx Usually green, outer part of a flower, formed from the sepals, that encases the petals in bud.
Classification Botanically and for ease of identification, plants are grouped according to family, genus, species and variety or cultivar. For example, with the rose family, *Rosaceae*, *Rosa* = genus, *R. gallica* = species, *R.g. var. officinalis* = variety, and *R.g.* 'Versicolor' = hybrid or cultivar.
Climber Plant that uses other plants or objects to grow upwards. Without support, their (usually) lax stems will creep along the ground.
Corm A swollen stem base that acts as a storage organ, similar to a bulb, but of a single piece without layers; it is annual, with the following year's corm developing from a bud close to the original.
Crown The part of a herbaceous plant from where new stems are produced and to where they die back in autumn.
Cultivar A man-made or cultivated variety, produced by hybridization. It will usually have a name chosen by the breeder, e.g. *Clematis* 'Bill Mackenzie'.
Cutting A section of a plant removed for propagation. Cuttings may be root, basal (new growth taken from a herbaceous plant in spring), greenwood (taken from the tip of young growth), softwood (young growth taken at the start of the growing season), semi-ripe (half-ripened stem taken during the growing season), or hardwood (mature stem taken at the end of the growing season).

D

Deciduous Plant losing its leaves annually; semi-deciduous plants lose some of their leaves.
Division Splitting of a plant clump into parts containing roots and shoots; normally done when the plant is dormant, for propagation.
Double flowers Applied to a flowerhead or bloom having more petals than the original species, e.g. *Bellis perennis* 'Alba Plena', a double version of the common daisy.

E

Evergreen Plant retaining its leaves at the end of the growing season, though older leaves may be lost through the year.

F

Family See classification.
Flowerhead Mass of small flowers that appear as one flower.

G

Gazebo Ornamental garden structure, usually of wood or iron, used as a raised viewing platform.
Genus see Classification
Glaucous Covered in a bluish-grey, bluish-green or bluish-white bloom.

H

Half-hardy Plant that withstands low temperatures but not freezing.
Harden off Allowing greenhouse-raised plants gradually to acclimatize to outside conditions by leaving them out for increasing periods before planting out.
Hardy Plant that tolerates year-round conditions in temperate climates, including normal frost, without protection.
Herbaceous Non-woody plant that dies down to its rootstock in winter.
Humus Largely decomposed organic matter naturally present in or introduced into the top layer of soil; improves soil fertility and water-holding capacity.
Hybrid A plant resulting from crossing two different species, often of the same genus, usually by cultivation, but sometimes occurring in the wild. An F1 hybrid is a plant that is propagated using the seed from two true parent plants, after hand-pollinating. Plants raised from hybrid seed (including F1 hybrids) often do not breed true to type.

I

Inflorescence A group or arrangement of flowers on a stem, such as panicles and racemes.
Intercrop A fast-growing crop grown between rows of a later and slower crop, e.g. lettuces between onions.

K

Knot garden Ornamental ground pattern of low hedging, infilled with planting or hard materials; intricate interweaving of the linear planting was a favourite device of Tudor and Elizabethan gardens.

M

Marginal Plant that grows partially submerged in shallow water or moist soil at a pond edge.
Micro-climate Normally refers to small area protected from extreme weather and so experiencing different climatic conditions from its locality. Micro-climates can be created, for example, by walls.
Mulch Layer of organic or inorganic material added to the surface of the soil to retain moisture, help suppress weeds and gradually improve fertility.

O

Offset Plant that is reproduced naturally from the base of the parent plant.

P

Panicle A flower stem (inflorescence) that branches into several small stems or stalks, with the youngest flowers at the top, e.g. lilac.
Perennial A plant that lives for longer than two seasons.
Picotee A *dianthus* (pink) having light petals edged with a darker colour.

R

Raceme A long, unbranched flower stem (inflorescence), the flowers opening in sequence from the bottom upwards.
Rhizome An underground, often creeping, stem acting as a storage organ, from which roots and shoots grow.
Root-ball The roots together with the soil adhering to them when a plant is lifted, e.g. for transplanting.

S

Sepals Green outer parts of a flower, collectively forming the calyx.
Single flowers Applied to a flower that has the normal number of petals for its species, such as a daisy.
Species See classification.
Standard A tree or shrub with a length of bare stem below the first branches; some shrubs, e.g. roses and fuschias, can be trained to form standards.

T

Topiary The art of clipping evergreen shrubs into specific shapes – such as cubes, pyramids or spheres.
Type Used to refer to an original plant species.

V

Variety A variant of a plant species, arising either naturally or as a result of selection.

INDEX

ACKNOWLEDGEMENTS

**The photographer, publishers and authors would like to thank the following
people and organizations who kindly allowed us to photograph their gardens:**
Don Brant; Tom & Jo Frosdick and their neighbours; Leeann MacKenzie; Jan Scruton.

**The authors and publishers are also grateful to the following for
their help and support in the production of this book:**
Val Bradley for the text for the Plant Finder; Lisa Dyer, Lisa Pendreigh and Sorcha Hitchcox for
editorial help; Dr Peter Boyce, Tony Lord and Brian Matthew for help with plant
checking and identification.

Suppliers of containers, plants, tools and equipment:
Granville Garden Centre, Granville Road, London NW2

Picture credits:
All photographs Collins & Brown copyright except the following:
(T = top; B= bottom; R = right; L = left; C= centre; M = middle)

Garden Picture Library: p. 6 (John Glover); p. 12 (John Glover); p. 26 (Juliet Wade); p. 27
(BR - Marie O'Hara); p. 61 (TR - Robert Estall) & (B - Juliet Wade); p. 74 (CL - Lamontagne);
p. 82 (Lynne Brotchie); p. 84 (Marie O'Hara); p. 85 (Linda Burgess); p. 90 (BR - Lynne Brotchie);
p. 94 (Friedrich Strauss); p. 95 (TR - Friedrich Strauss & BR - Linda Burgess).

Michelle Garrett: p. 54 (BL); p. 68 (TR, BL); p. 69; p. 98 (TR); p. 122 (TL).

**Collins & Brown Limited would like to thank the following photographers
for taking the following photographs:**
Michelle Garrett: p. 14; p. 15; p. 16; p. 17; p. 18; p. 19; p. 20; p. 21; p. 22; p. 23; p. 28; p. 29; p. 32 (TL,
CR); p. 33; p. 34; p. 35 (TR); p. 36 (TL); p. 37 (TL, TR, BR); p. 38; p. 39; p. 40; p. 41; p. 42; p. 43; p.
44; p. 46 (BL); p. 47 (TL, BR); p. 48 (BR); p. 51; p. 52 (TR); p. 53 (TR); p 56 (BL); p. 57; p. 58; p. 62;
p. 63; p. 64; p. 65; p. 66; p. 67; p. 68 (TL); p. 70; p. 71 (TL, TR, BL); p. 72; p. 73; p. 74 (BL); p. 76; p.
77; p. 78; p. 79; p. 80 (TL, TM; BL); p. 81; p. 83; p. 86 (CM, CR, BM); p. 87; p. 88 (BL); p. 89; p. 90
(TR); p. 91; p. 96; p. 97; p. 99; p. 100; p. 101; p. 102; p. 103; p. 105; p. 106 (BL, BR); p. 107 (BL); p.
108 (TR, BL, BM); p. 109 (TM, TR, BL, BM); p. 110 (CR, BL, BM, BR); p. 111 (TR, BR); p. 112
(BR); p. 115 (BR); p .116 (BL); p. 117 (TL, TR, CR); p. 130 (TL); p. 136 (TL).

Howard Rice: p. 50 (BR); p. 114 (BR); p. 119; p. 121; p. 122 (BM, BR); p. 123 (CM, BM, BR); p. 125
(TL, TM, TR, CR); p. 126; p. 127 (TR, CR); p. 128 (TL, TR, CR); p. 129; p. 130 (BR); p. 131; p. 132;
p. 133 (T2ndL, T2ndR, CL); p. 134; p. 135; p. 136 (BM, BR); p. 137.

Steven Wooster: p. 1; p. 2; p. 7; p. 8; p. 9; p. 10; p. 11; p. 13; p. 24; p. 25; p. 27 (TL); p. 30; p. 31; p. 32
(BL); p. 35 (B); p. 36 (BR); p. 37 (BL); p. 45; p. 49; p. 50 (TR); p. 55; p. 56 (BR); p. 59; p. 60; p. 75; p.
88 (TL); p. 92; p. 93; p. 98 (BM); p. 118; p. 123 (CR, BL): p. 124; p. 127 (TL, TM, CM, BR); p. 128
(TM); p. 133 (TL, TR, CR).